PRAISE FOR *WORDS*

As the CEO of my own STREAM foundation and creator of STEM-based cooking classes and workshops, the advice in this book is super valuable. It is full of new ways of how to put your customers at the heart of your company, manage your external media relationships, and lead with purpose, heart, and passion. As a 16-year-old business owner, *Words That Work* gives me the playbook for continuing to grow my business to new heights! Your work, advice, and tools are priceless information for any business entrepreneur.

Simone Bridges, CEO, Goddess Food Factory, Founder, Simone Bridges Inspires Inc.

Val Wright has made the ultimate guide to business communication. *Words That Work* is full of suggestions and alternative statements that open up communication. I am excited to have this new tool that will help me improve my ability to ask questions and affirm what others are saying.

Rachel Canales, Chief of Staff, Global Accounts and Chief Customer Advocate, Lenovo

Val Wright has been an immensely valuable strategic advisor to me surrounding innovation and leadership through acquisitions and an IPO. I have considered her previous books required reading for any executive responsible for leading people through growth and change, and her clear, insightful voice will put her new book on the top of my recommended reading list. In her characteristic style, Wright provides candid advice every leader needs to navigate innovation, communicate with impact, harness emotions, and actively manage external and internal communications. The easy-to-read format addresses the many situations executives will go through when they are asked to create outcomes that stretch beyond the current trajectory of the business.

John Schneider, Chief Marketing Officer, Betterworks

Val Wright's third book sets us on a path to the essential art of truth-telling in business. I've used Wright's words in many situations and it's true, they do just work! The practical examples in this book will allow every leader to speak more boldly, which will grow their business and career.

Susan Potter, Vice President of Digital Experience, Hootsuite

This book is a culmination of the wise counsel Val Wright has given me over the last few years. Just the right words at the exact right moment. Every leader needs to read this book and benefit from its confidence-building positivity. The world needs to hear from more incredible, badass, uplifting women like Val Wright.

Ronalee Zarate-Bayani, Chief Marketing Officer, Newlight Technologies

Words That Work

Communicate Your Purpose, Your Profits and Your Performance

Val Wright

KoganPage

First published in Great Britain and the United States in 2022 by Kogan Page Limited

2nd Floor, 45 Gee Street
London
EC1V 3RS
United Kingdom

8 W 38th Street, Suite 902
New York, NY 10018
USA

4737/23 Ansari Road
Daryaganj
New Delhi 110002
India

www.koganpage.com

Kogan Page books are printed on paper from sustainable forests.

ISBNs
Hardback   978 1 3986 0333 2
Paperback   978 1 3986 0330 1
Ebook   978 1 3986 0331 8

British Library Cataloguing-in-Publication Data
A CIP record for this book is available from the British Library.

Library of Congress Cataloging-in-Publication Data
Names: Wright, Val, 1974– author.
Title: Words that work: communicate your purpose, your profits and your
    performance / Val Wright.
Description: London, United Kingdom; New York, NY: Kogan Page, 2022. |
    Includes bibliographical references and index.
Identifiers: LCCN 2021049021 (print) | LCCN 2021049022 (ebook) | ISBN
    9781398603301 (paperback) | ISBN 9781398603332 (hardback) | ISBN
    9781398603318 (ebook)
Subjects: LCSH: Communication in management. | Business communication.
Classification: LCC HD30.3 .W76 2022 (print) | LCC HD30.3 (ebook) | DDC
    658.4/5–dc23/eng/20211006
LC record available at https://lccn.loc.gov/2021049021
LC ebook record available at https://lccn.loc.gov/2021049022

Typeset by Integra Software Services, Pondicherry
Print production managed by Jellyfish
Printed and bound by CPI Group (UK) Ltd, Croydon CR0 4YY

To the incredible families that supported our family throughout the 2020 global pandemic. The Novaks, the Coopers, and the Shirreffs, we were so fortunate to have you in our bubble!

CONTENTS

LIST OF FIGURES AND TABLES

ABOUT THE AUTHOR

Internationally acclaimed innovation and growth expert Val Wright was named as one of the top 50 resources for chief operating officers by ClickSoftware. She is one of only 64 experts inducted into the Million Dollar Consultant® Hall of Fame.

The global clients who have requested her help include Starbucks, LinkedIn, Amazon, francesca's, Microsoft, the *Financial Times*, Seagate, Gartner, and the LA Lakers. Val's corporate experience includes tenures during dramatic growth periods at Amazon, BMW, Microsoft, Harrods, and Xbox.

Val participated in the small team that created the fastest-selling device of all time, Kinect for Xbox, which won a Guinness World Record, selling over 20 million devices. This contributed to the turnaround of Microsoft's entertainment business from a billion-dollar loss to a multimillion-dollar profit machine.

Her unique approach, which she has trademarked as Thoughtfully Ruthless®, has produced typical client results of market domination in extraordinarily short time frames along with compassionate truth-telling, fearlessness, and extensive creative, technical, and leadership gains.

Val's books include *Thoughtfully Ruthless: The key to exponential growth*—named UK Amazon best-selling time management skills book, best business book by the Independent Press Awards and NYC Big Book Awards, and best career book by the Book Excellence Awards—and *Rapid Growth, Done Right: Lead, influence, and innovate for success*, which was named best business book by NYC Big Book Awards. Val is a regular contributor for CNBC, *The Wall Street Journal*, BBC News, Fox Business, *Inc. Magazine*, *Business Insider*, *Fast Company*, Bloomberg, Reuters, the *Los Angeles Times*, MSN, and *Today*.

Originally from England, Val now lives in California with her three daughters and husband.

ACKNOWLEDGMENTS

This has been my favorite book to write of all three of my books because I could share exactly the most popular advice CEOs and executives tell me works. What was initially a paragraph in a previous book could never have blossomed into its own book without the support of the following people.

I could never have written it without the fortune of working with brilliant global executives who I learn from just as much as I help.

For the last three years, John Schneider has been persistent in telling me that I must write this book as we worked together. I appreciate your tenacity!

Chris Cudmore, Martin Hill, Jaini Haria, Vanessa Rueda, Nancy Wallace, Heather Langridge, Zexna Opara, and the brilliant team at Kogan Page, your wise advice and guidance has resulted in a book I cannot wait to get into the hands of every leader possible!

Finally, my husband, Andy, for sending me off to Palm Springs for a week when he could tell I needed to escape homeschooling our daughters and just simply write.

PREFACE

When a Broadway or West End show opens, every cast member knows their lines. When it is time for the Super Bowl, World Cup, or Grand Slam, the athletes have prepared with precision. Yet in boardrooms, strategy retreats, and conference rooms around the world, leaders are starting off ill-prepared for conversations that have millions of dollars of investments at stake. Too often, leaders endlessly fact-check financial data and spend far too long deciding which font or graphic to use in a presentation slide, all to the detriment of preparing exactly what they are going to say. Sharing exact phrases that have been used by CEOs and senior executives from world-leading companies including Starbucks, Microsoft, Amazon, and BMW, *Words That Work* gives leaders the playbook for successful conversations in critical business scenarios.

As a CEO or senior executive, the stakes are extraordinary in every conversation. Millions or even billions of dollars are in jeopardy during board meetings, investor calls, media interviews, customer interactions and employee conversations. The most successful executives know this and invest their time preparing in a thoughtful and intentional way while continuously improving their knowledge and skills in how to communicate to drive profitable growth.

Emerging from a global pandemic and societal awakenings requires new skills in communication. Familiar approaches for interacting with customers, employees and investors need to be turned on their side to be questioned, challenged and changed.

Throughout this book we will pause and deconstruct words that work and words that do not work. I will give you a rapid list of alternative words to say in a multitude of situations. If you have an inattentive brain like mine, skip to the appendix where you can find the shortcut to the complete list of actual phrases and words that simply work.

This book is designed to be read as a choose your own adventure style of discovery. You do not need to read it in order from Chapter 1 through Chapter 12. Pick a chapter that most appeals to you and start there. Flip through and look at the pictures and pause on what seems most interesting. If you prefer writing notes as you follow along, go to www.wrightwordsthatjustwork.com and download the accompanying workbook so you can insert your commentary, progress, and reflections.

In my book *Rapid Growth, Done Right*, I shared two stories, the first about how a CIO was presenting to the board and asked for my advice. In this story, I explained how my three principles of Words That Just Work are purpose, preparation, and practice, and I provided advice for just what to say and when to say it. We discussed the script, precise questions to ask, and exact phrases to use. The second story was another client who got to practice a conversation in preparation for a one-on-one with her divisional president. She was frustrated that the promises about promotion when she was hired were not being fulfilled as fast as she hoped. She practiced, had the conversation, and the following week was told the size of her team would be doubled. This mattered because her president was going on sabbatical, and had she not had the conversation, it would not have happened for at least six months.

As I wrote about those stories in that book, I provided a bonus to readers by offering complimentary Words That Just Work advice for every reader's situation. I told readers they could contact me via text message and explain their situation and the results they wanted to achieve. Then I would provide advice on words that will just work. As a result, I received hundreds of texts from around the world asking for specific scenario advice. I even had many leaders ask me if I would dedicate a whole book on the topic, which ultimately led me to writing this book.

Now, as you read this book I am sure you will think of scenarios unique to you, so again, I am extending the invite to readers here.

> **BONUS FEATURE**
>
> As a special bonus for every reader, I offer you complimentary Words That Just Work advice for one situation. You can text me by entering your cell phone number at www.textvalnow.com. You will receive a message back saying I have received your number. Let me know your name and then you can text me your situation and the results you want to achieve. I will provide you with words that just work.

By reading this book, you too can benefit from the strategies, language and tools of CEOs and executives who have been there, said this, and delivered remarkable results. With the help of this essential guide born out of my personal experience with the most powerful executives in the world, you will never forget your lines again. Now watch your performance and your profits hit new heights.

01

Creating a Company of Truth Tellers

Do you really know if everyone around you is being honest with you?

No one wants to be lied to, yet untruths are everywhere. No one wants to admit they may occasionally lie, but they hypocritically expect everyone else to always tell the truth. Growing up, I was told white lies are okay if they prevent someone's feelings being hurt, but when do little white lies turn big and dangerous? Just like the American TV show *Big Little Lies* featuring Reese Witherspoon and Nicole Kidman, the little lies can rapidly spiral out of control with disastrous consequences.

"That's not what I ordered; I wanted a latte," Adam Konran, editor of *Forbes* magazine, told the barista at WeWork's corporate head-quarters in 2015.[1] "Oh, we call lattes cappuccinos, and cappuccinos lattes, around here!" the barista enthusiastically replied, much to Konran's surprise. Why the coffee confusion? It all began when WeWork CEO Adam Neumann insisted that his preferred coffee drink was called a latte, when he actually wanted a cappuccino. Did anyone tell him the truth, correct him, and explain his mistake? Absolutely not. Instead, the barista and all the employees at the head-quarters renamed the coffee drinks to fit with what Neumann incorrectly believed they were called based on his preference of frothy foam versus steamed milk.

This almost unbelievable tale is the modern-day version of the emperor who has no clothes. Not one single person at WeWork felt they could tell Neumann the truth about coffee. Instead, it became a widespread part of the WeWork culture of drink ordering. Every time any intern, new employee, senior executive, or visitor ordered a coffee, they played along, changing the name, explaining to those not in the know the façade that had been built because of their CEO. Which begs the question, if they were dishonest about coffee, what else were they covering up or lying about?

This chapter helps you distinguish between the truth and a well-intended lie. It provides inside access to CEOs who have been lied to and how they were able to create a company where contagious truth telling led to profit and revenue beyond everyone's expectations. It also includes a toolkit to help you speak your mind without worrying about what you will say and how it will be received. It reviews the biggest little lies in recent corporate history and why they matter, and we start your Words That Work journey at the most crucial point, making sure you are being told the truth, can share the truth, and know how to spot a lie.

CHAPTER TOPICS

- Start with the CEO
- Speaking Your Mind Without Minding What You Say
- Creating a Contagious Truth-Telling Company
- Demolishing the Executive Insulation Layer
- Pause Game: Play Game
- Defining and Sharing What Your Company Really Cares About
- Additional Rapid Truth-Telling Words That Work

The way you react to the truth is contagious; you will spread either endless truth telling, or slowly people will realize that you don't actually want to know what they think, so they will avoid, cover up, or just blindly agree with whatever you say. It is easy to use hindsight to connect the WeWork coffee incident to their ultimate financial crisis, but small things lead to larger patterns. The WeWork saga didn't stop at coffee confusion. The information avoidance and the lack of clarity on its true company impact and results is well documented. Just like well-known corporate scandals involving Wells Fargo and Volkswagen, the common cause is this: no one felt they were able to tell the truth. So exactly how do you create and maintain a place to work where speaking up and speaking out is okay?

Start with the CEO

It always starts at the top, and that's especially so for truth telling. If you are the CEO reading this, you are in the best possible spot to influence truth telling in your company. If not, it's still possible to make an impact, but the road to ultimate truth telling will be a little longer.

When WeWork was valued at $47 billion in 2017, it wasn't clear who was trying to tell the truth, but if you watch Hulu's documentary *WeWork: The making and breaking of a $47 billion unicorn*, you will see plenty of hindsight truth telling. This is so much easier to do after the fact, when you are no longer being paid by the very company you are talking about!

The foundation of the astronomical value was based on the belief that WeWork was a technology company, and its astronomical value was based on anything but truth telling. The unfortunate reality was that it was in the real estate business, dressing itself up as a technology company to attract that valuation. The exact basis of that technology company valuation was revealed by interviews in the Hulu documentary; it was a much-hyped, little-used internal social network. Former employees revealed that the social network was pitched to investors as the heart of the company and a key unique differentiator. But the reality was that very few people actually used it. So the coffee confusion was the canary in a coal mine. Many of the WeWork investors would surely have loved to know sooner than they actually did.

You are likely wondering, how exactly do you avoid that delusional view of your company performance and how you show this to the outside world?

"I'll be blunt, because I know no other way.**"**

That is my typical introduction when an executive asks for my opinion and we don't know each other. Those who know me know that's exactly what they will get, and usually that is precisely why they want to keep working with me. I won't filter, fluff, skirt, caveat, dilute, couch, or hide my opinion because that is just what CEOs and senior executives need—honesty. After all, I am just giving my opinion. I always clarify if it's based on observed behavior, data I've reviewed, or feedback I've heard from others, or whether it's not statistically significant, or just simply a hunch. I always share; that's the unique value that I bring to advising executives and companies as an external strategy and growth expert. The big question for you as you read this is whether you have people around you who speak just as bluntly and freely. It's possible you are impacted by the Truth-Telling Fallacy.

Truth-Telling Fallacy

In my corporate work life at Microsoft, BMW, Amazon, and Marconi, I found the Truth-Telling Fallacy to be the most frustrating

FIGURE 1.1 Truth-Telling Fallacy

part of business life. It became clearer as I rose through the corporate ranks, but I found it everywhere—from larger international
companies to family-run businesses and privately held companies.
The Truth-Telling Fallacy affects businesses of every size, impacting
senior executives, managers, and teams alike. Here are the five
factors in play:

1. THE MORE SENIOR YOU RISE, FEWER PEOPLE TELL YOU THE TRUTH

If you're a CEO or at the top of the organization, think back to
earlier in your career. Remember how much feedback and real talk
you had about your performance? Did you notice that start to evapo-
rate throughout your career as you got promoted?

"I need your unfiltered advice on this acquisition strategy, Val."

That is what one CEO client called me to say as she was reviewing
two potential acquisitions as part of the company's growth plan. She
had not been with the company long and was still changing its truth-
telling (or lack thereof!) culture, and they needed a blunt assessment.
There is unique value in having external unfiltered advice, but as a
leader your real opportunity is unlocking it internally, because sadly,
too many people are afraid to give senior people the truth.

2. THOSE AT THE TOP OF THE COMPANY NEED THE MOST FEEDBACK

I've been in far too many product reviews, board discussions, and
leadership meetings where the attendees could be replaced with those
bobble-head figures that are given out before sports games! If these
executive gatherings are not truth-telling opportunities, where exactly
are senior leaders supposed to get their truth telling and straight-up
feedback?

3. YOU NEED TO BE COMFORTABLE WITH BEING UNCOMFORTABLE

It is not easy to hear truth telling. It can be awkward, difficult, and even
painful to receive. Not everyone has the knowledge, skills, or mindset
to get comfortable with these feelings. Throughout this book you will

learn specific tools to use, words to quote, and preparation to follow to receive such feedback. The greatest news is that this is all teachable, but the tough news is that the greatest barrier to changing here is *you*.

4. COMPANIES INVERSELY SPEND ALL THEIR TIME ON TRUTH TELLING IN THE WRONG PLACES

Billions in resources each year are spent on training across companies. Unfortunately, the majority of this is spent in the most junior ranks of the company, when the opposite is needed with top teams, the CEO, and the board. Figure 1.1 shows that actual truth telling is inversely proportioned to the need for truth telling. Similarly, the investment in giving those who need it help with changing the level of truth telling is spent in the wrong place. When I talk about training and development here, for any investment, I don't mean bland instruction or click-happy online guides, but true intentional investment in time, accountability, and resources for how to create a truth-telling company. In Chapter 2 you will learn how to raise the performance bar of your teams, in Chapter 8 you will learn how to unlock the power of your board, and finally in Chapter 11 you will receive the playbook of tools to make all this happen.

5. TRUTH TELLING NEEDS TO BE REWARDED

The final, and perhaps most critical, factor in creating a truth-telling company is how you reward truth telling. The much-critiqued Fyre Festival of 2017 had everybody fooled that there really would be a celebrity-packed luxury holiday with headline musicians and exclusive accommodations. The reality was that it was a disastrous, food-starved, cheap camping trip without any entertainment. When Netflix and Amazon filmed their exposé documentaries, hindsight whistleblowers came out in full force. I've seen CEOs publicly thank truth tellers who point out mistakes they have made. Amazon has a leadership principle named *has backbone*. During my corporate career on the Amazon fashion leadership team, you could not be promoted to a manager, director, or vice president if your immediate manager could not give strong evidence that you had displayed backbone with those more senior than you.

Speaking Your Mind Without Minding What You Say

How well does your company value, call out, recognize and reward truth telling? We will now explore how to evaluate how well you and the rest of your company can speak your mind without minding what you say.

The Truth-Telling Test

I've used the truth-telling test with companies all around the world. It is a baseline for accelerating innovation and growth because new ideas won't fly if you can't be direct with each other.

RATE EACH QUESTION

1: Strongly disagree

2: Disagree

3: Neither agree nor disagree

4: Agree

5: Strongly agree

Part A—About You

1 I'm regularly given good/mediocre/ugly news in a timely manner.

2 I seek out contrarian reviews and enthusiastically receive them even if it is uncomfortable.

3 I am told when my ideas won't work or when there is a better alternative.

4 There is healthy disagreement in my executive team discussions.

5 I actively encourage, coach, and reward truth telling in teams I lead.

Part B—Your Immediate Manager

1 It is easy for me to give good/mediocre/ugly news to my immediate manager.

2 My immediate manager seeks out contrarian views to their own and enthusiastically receives them even when uncomfortable.

3 I tell my immediate manager when the ideas won't work or there is a better alternative.

4 There is healthy disagreement in my immediate manager's team discussions.

5 My immediate manager actively encourages coaches and rewards truth telling in the team they lead.

Part C—Your Company

1 Across the company it is easy to give good/mediocre/ugly news to other functions.

2 Other leaders seek out contrarian views to their own and enthusiastically receive them even when uncomfortable.

3 I tell other functions and teams when the ideas won't work or there is a better alternative.

4 There is healthy disagreement across team and function discussions.

5 Managers across the company encourage coaches and reward truth telling in the team they lead.

CALCULATING YOUR TRUTH-TELLING SCORE

First take your score for each section and calculate your truth-telling percentage scores for each section and overall.

TABLE 1.1   Your Truth-Telling Score

	Score	%
A: I am an exemplar of truth telling	/25	
B: My immediate manager is an exemplar	/25	
C: Our company demonstrates truth telling	/25	
Our Contagious Truth-Telling Score	/75	

Now total your score:

- **>80% Truth-Telling Exemplar**—Congratulations! You have mastered creating a team where you can receive truth-telling feedback.

There may be some individual questions to focus on, but use this opportunity to teach your teams and your peers how to receive truth telling as well as you do by encouraging them to consider the questions and discuss opportunities for increased truth telling.

- **41–79% Truth-Telling Opportunities**—You have areas where you may have an insulation layer around you. Identify which are causing you the greatest pain or those that are the quickest to change. Read on for tools and ideas to break down that insulation layer. Once initial changes are in place, pick another two, focus on those, and continue until you are satisfied.

- **<40% In the Dark**—Watch out: you are in a cave, only hearing your own echo! Perhaps you have just taken over a team, joined a new company, or there are broader dynamics at play. Talk through your results with someone you trust and build a fast plan for addressing the top two areas of concern for you. Keep reading for some immediate actions to help you.

FIGURE 1.2   Truth-Telling Triangle

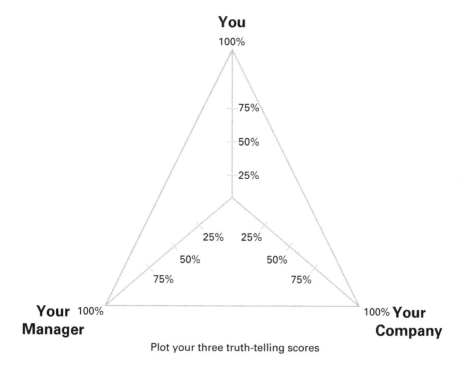

You may choose to only look at your results, or you may choose to extend to your whole team. The most powerful work I get to do is when the truth-telling reflection occurs across every function and location. I created the Truth-Telling Triangle in Figure 1.2 to let you visually see the comparisons between you, your manager, and the company's expectations vs. reality on truth telling. By plotting the individual percentage scores you can see the pattern of where there are similarities. You can now begin to understand the dynamic in play, depending on whether your truth telling is aligned with that of your boss and your company.

By now you may be beginning to realize what it means to work in a contagious truth-telling company. Perhaps you have experienced one, or parts of one. If you have ever felt the ultimate freedom to say what you are thinking without concern for backlash or retribution, have confidence to ask for and receive the truth no matter how difficult, and have seen senior leaders role-model and reward speaking your mind, then you have experienced a contagious truth-telling company. Let's explore the journey of one company.

Creating a Contagious Truth-Telling Company

Andrew Clarke became CEO of womenswear retailer francesca's ten days before the 2020 global pandemic Covid-19 hit and created the resulting financial crisis. Surprisingly, there was another significant threat to the business that Clarke had to contend with: a severe lack of truth telling across the company's 711 boutiques and 5,000 associates. As the seventh CEO in nine years, Clarke inherited a company that had suffered from a revolving door of executives and the dizzy, confusing results of continuous changes in strategy and decisions. I use the Contagious Truth-Telling Scale shown in Figure 1.3 to allow leaders and companies to map where they are and how they can rise past each door to the next level of truth telling without falling back down into the dark again.

When Clarke took over, francesca's was at Stage One: **In the Dark** on the Contagious Truth-Telling scale shown in Figure 1.3. Nobody

FIGURE 1.3   Contagious Truth-Telling Scale

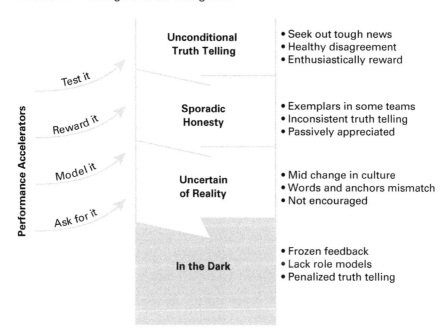

spoke up, and associates in boutiques had highly scripted words to use when customers arrived to shop for an outfit. Meetings had pre-meetings, and participation was choreographed with extreme precision and all spontaneous ideas and feedback were suffocated.

Clarke followed the Performance Accelerators for Contagious Truth Telling for reaching that aspirational level of Unconditional Truth Telling at the top of the scale by asking for it, modeling it, rewarding it, and testing it. This moved francesca's into Stage Two of the Contagious Truth-Telling Scale: **Uncertain of Reality**. Initial reactions were similar to when you visit a new country and the social rules are completely the opposite to what you are used to: there was an awkwardness as everyone figured out what was safe and acceptable.

The third stage of Contagious Truth Telling is **Sporadic Honesty**. This is where certain functions, locations, or levels of seniority are demonstrating truth telling, but it is not yet widespread.

The ultimate goal is Stage Four: **Unconditional Truth Telling,** which cannot be rushed, faked, or underestimated.

Demolishing the Executive Insulation Layer

Who a CEO chooses to hire also has the potential to suffocate truth telling. It's not uncommon for executives to hire people who are like them, people from the same college, those they have worked with before, and those skewed to their functional expertise. If a CEO is highly technical, they might value and hire those who have a stronger technical background, or are from technology-forward companies, but may not value the creative experts as much. The same can happen with those with a deep financial background, which can also create an imbalance where it's easy to just dive into topics and strategies that are familiar without hearing contrarian points of view. This is where you create a dangerous insulation layer that can stop the truth from being told and explored.

How exactly do you convince leaders to listen to this? First, you have to look beyond the CEO to the board and to external advisors who are working with the top executive team and determine whether there are people who are willing to speak up and point things out. More important, you have to determine whether those people are listened to and if there is a willingness to change.

When top executives operate with a buffer zone that deflects the truth, I call that the **insulation layer**.

Thinking about this, you probably know an executive who has surrounded themselves in this insulation layer. Their behavior suggests that they don't want to hear that they have this layer. Or if you do tell them, they will act in a way that means you're absolutely never going to tell them anything contrarian ever again!

For truth telling to become truly contagious, every dimension needs to be exemplary, from your CEO and board to advisors, executives, managers, and teams. You can use the Truth-Telling Progress Tracker in Figure 1.4 to create a rapid snapshot of truth telling across your company. You can rate with a simple + for positive, – for negative, and ? when you

FIGURE 1.4   Truth-Telling Progress Tracker

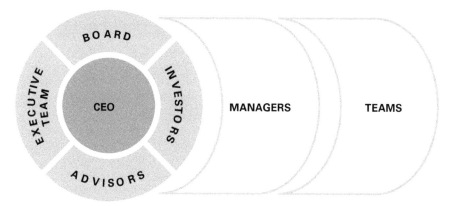

Rating
+ Consistent demonstration of truth telling
– Lack of or inconsistent truth telling
? Unknown level of truth telling

are not sure. This lets you evaluate and monitor where contagious truth telling exists in your company. As you work through the ideas in this book, you can come back and update your progress. For electronic copies of this tool and all the others in this book, visit www.wrightwordsthatwork.com to download them.

At francesca's, a new executive joined Andrew Clarke a few weeks later as SVP, Merchandising and supported the increased level of truth telling across the company. Victoria Taylor became an exemplar of truth telling, which became the bar for her peers. This could be because she had worked with Clarke previously when he was president of Kmart apparel, so she had more confidence than her peers to challenge a newly appointed CEO. One of my favorite examples of Words That Work emerged when Taylor questioned a particular strategy:

"Does anyone else think we are doing this in the wrong order?**"**

WORDS THAT WORK DECONSTRUCTION

Taking this simple sentence, I am going to explain why this is powerful.

- Rather than simply saying, "You are doing this wrong," a question invites others to see the situation through a different lens.

- It causes a powerful pause, not to determine who is right and who is wrong, but for a thoughtful consideration of an alternative way of approaching it

- It encourages debate, not dissent. A healthy truth-telling company is comfortable with debate, and that is exactly what Taylor created by using these powerful Words That Work.

Author's truth-telling note

❝Let's pause this conversation to share some inner thoughts...❞

I would never have been able to write the previous paragraph when I wrote my first book, *Thoughtfully Ruthless*, in 2015, or my second book, *Rapid Growth, Done Right*, in 2019. At the time, I was unaware that I had a neurodiverse brain, or that the way I think was different, unique, or needed a different level of care and treatment. I have spent the last two years telling my story of my discovery of my ADHD brain, and it has caused me to pause to really ask how others like to communicate, process information, and learn. It was one of my favorite clients, Rachel Canales, Chief of Staff at Lenovo, who kept telling me for about three months that I should really create a workbook for those who hate to write in books but would love to process their thoughts in writing as they reflect and learn. I am grateful for Rachel's endless truth telling, and full credit for the development of the workbook goes to her. Why is this reflection important on a meta level? Because there isn't just content learning here for you, there is learning for all of us, including me; we need to have people around who share new ideas that allow us to challenge how we are approaching our work, question our conventions, and cause us to pause and reflect on our ways of working.

The last meta-level reflection is this: How are you providing your own author's notes to your team? You have to rise above your current discussions and observe your team as though you are watching a play at the theater, and you are in the balcony seats watching it all play out.

Pause Game: Play Game

Truth telling is most valuable in the moment, but you really need to pause the actual action in progress for it to be effective. The Pause Game: Play Game approach is a simple but clever technique that allows you to freeze what is currently happening and share insights as an observer. I first learned the technique when I overheard my three young daughters playing a game involving Princess Leia, a dinosaur, and a unicorn. Midway through the game, one said, "Wait, pause game! I don't want to be Princess Leia anymore. I want to be Yoda, but the dinosaur and Yoda have to be kind to each other. Play game!" This happened many times when one daughter didn't like how the game wasn't going in her favor, or didn't like what was said or the way it was said.

The following week I was leading a strategy session with a Starbucks executive team when there was a particularly heated exchange that was incredibly circular and ineffective. It occurred to me on the spot that they might learn something from the way my daughters play together! I needed them to pause and deconstruct what was happening. But, in true truth-telling form for you reading this, I was a little apprehensive about relating a story about my kids and Yoda while working with a team responsible for billions of dollars of impact. So I decided to try it using words I hoped would work.

I used a key phrase for interjecting in a heated debate:

"As I listen to you all, it occurred to me..."

WORDS THAT WORK DECONSTRUCTION

This interjection works for three reasons:

- By starting with explaining that I was listening, I indicated that I cared, which often puts people at ease in tense situations.

- By using the reference *you all*, I indicated inclusivity rather than calling out one specific individual.

- Uttering the words *it occurred to me* allowed me to forewarn those listening that I was about to make a key observation before jumping in and reporting that observation. Our brains often need time to adjust from being in a heated debate to being ready to reflect and consider alternative views.

Back to the Starbucks executive conference room: I explained the Pause Game: Play Game approach and how my daughters play together, and I asked them the next reflective question:

"Who wants to go first sharing their observations on this conversation?"

This allowed everyone to stop debating the strategic decision and comment on the dynamic in the room. We switched from a content conversation to a process conversation. By asking who wanted to go first, I indicated that this wasn't a question of if but of when this would be discussed. The conversation uncovered confusion, incorrect assumptions, and misinformation on the goals they were collectively trying to achieve. It also became clear that there were some previous difficult conversations that had never been resolved. The shift that happened in that conversation was quite remarkable. At the time I reflected on all the previous contentious conversations that had not been confronted or deconstructed, or had been left to simmer in previous meetings. You can only imagine the delight when I returned home from my trip and shared with my daughters how their game had helped some of my clients.

I have used the Pause Game: Play Game technique over 100 times since. As I sit writing this on the plane home from a different executive retreat, I have used it again to acknowledge positive interactions that the team was displaying and was able to validate their success and progress by asking:

" That felt different to how you
typically interact, anyone else see that? **"**

Not all call-outs need to be negative. You often need to validate your progress and success to reinforce positive changes and acknowledge the journey you and your team are on. We will explore this further in Chapter 3.

Defining and Sharing What Your Company Really Cares About

"*Who are ya?!*" is a popular chant sung by British football fans at matches when they feel the opposing team is relatively insignificant. While I hope nobody has never sung or said that to you at work, you know some people you meet are thinking it. This is not particularly helpful and is judgmental.

I'll never forget my first business trip to BMW headquarters in Munich. I was working for Land Rover at the time, in the European Sales and Marketing Division, helping lead the cultural integration after BMW had acquired Land Rover and Mini. BMW wanted to make changes as the manufacturing sites were losing $3 million a day. As I arrived alongside the Land Rover EMEA president, we walked down a long wood-paneled corridor to the formal meeting room at the very end. We made our introductions and sat down, and one of our BMW colleagues looked and me and said, "Tea." I was very thirsty, so I was delighted at the offer and replied, "Yes please, milk no sugar, thank you." At the time I paid no attention to why the Land Rover president jumped up and got everyone tea. On the flight home my colleague explained the reality of what had happened. There was no question mark after the word tea; it had not been an offer, but an instruction to me, the only female in the room of twelve, to provide tea to everyone else in the room. Looking back now, I am relieved that I was a naïve twenty-four-year-old, oblivious to the offensive request. At the time I paid no attention to why the Land Rover president jumped up and got everyone tea, and it certainly was nowhere near a truth-telling culture where that observation could have been made.

Mission, vision, and company values are plastered across corporate hallways, annual reports, and websites' posters. Sadly, too often they are empty words, vacuous and glib promises. The reality is found in those meeting interactions, when the shiny promises in the hiring process dull and you get to see your real boss, your real company, and the reality of your company. Chapter 10 sets up how to have the perfect launch into any new role.

Additional Rapid Truth-Telling Words That Work

Preparing the conversation

"My intention here is to..."

"Is now a good time to share some thoughts or when would work?"

"Let me be blunt..."

"If I was truth telling I would simply say..."

"I am working on being more direct, so let me say..."

"Does anyone else think we are doing this in the wrong order?"

"I'd love to share my observations, is now a good time?"

Getting to the heart of the issue

"I have a contrarian point of view..."

"Does anyone else think we are doing this in the wrong order?"

"Here's how I experienced that..."

"I'd like to share a pattern I have noticed..."

"This is my initial impression, but I thought you would want to hear it..."

"I don't know if you have heard this from others..."

"When is the best time to share some thoughts with you?"

"I have concerns about this project that it is important for you to hear..."

"I have an alternative view than the rest of the team..."

"Before we go ahead may I share an alternative approach?"

"In the spirit of truth telling..."

"As we committed to truth telling, I am going to practice that now..."

"When we were in the last meeting, I am curious how you felt it went."

❝I'd love to hear if you thought
that conversation went as planned...**❞**

❝Did you think the team demonstrated
truth telling in that conversation?**❞**

❝May I share how I observed it?**❞**

Ending the conversation

❝I appreciate you listening and considering my point of view.**❞**

❝I appreciate that may have been
difficult to hear, but I wanted to share.**❞**

If the reaction doesn't go well

❝I'll give you some time to consider,
then let's continue the conversation.**❞**

The journey to creating a company of truth tellers is not an overnight transformation but one that requires thought, commitment, investment, and all of the tools provided in this chapter. Throughout this book you will learn additional tools for dealing successfully with all elements of your role so that you can truly unlock the power of Words That Work.

Now we have uncovered how to improve truth telling in your company, in Chapter 2 let's look at how to raise the performance bar for your team so that you can put some of the changes you want to make into action.

Bonus offer: For anyone reading this who isn't a CEO, I have a bonus offer for you. I will send a copy of this book as a gift from me to your CEO. Go to www.wrightwordsthatwork.com and send me a message with the title Truth Telling and I will give your CEO a copy of this book, which will then create an easier conversation starter with your CEO.

If you received this gift from someone in your company, then they have a reason they want you to see this book and likely this specific chapter. To understand why, you can simply ask them:

> **"**I am curious, what prompted you to give me this book? I'd love to hear.**"**

Endnote

1   Wilkinson, A (2021) Americans believe in work. WeWork preyed on that instinct, Vox https://www.vox.com/22358597/wework-documentary-hulu-neumann (archived at https://perma.cc/L3VE-QE7Q)

02

Setting the Right Hurdle Height

CEOs are the ultimate pacemakers, they set the bar for performance. They are also the referee to determine if the standard has been met and the points earned. This chapter provides the language, tools, and examples of how to make sure you are driving executive accountability and flawless execution as well as providing powerful feedback for those who don't meet your performance bar. It also explores what happens when mediocrity creeps up on you, or if helicopter leadership takes over, or if executive distancing occurs.

CHAPTER TOPICS

- The Control Fallacy
- The Right Height for Your Expectations
- The Art of Giving Feedback That Actually Changes Something
- Tracking Performance Progress
- Countdown to Your Best Year Yet
- Rapid Remarkable Performance Words That Work

In your career, the spotlight on you gets brighter as you ascend the corporate organization chart. More people are viewing what you do and cameras keep getting added covering every angle. It may feel like the whole world is watching, especially if you are a CEO, member of the board, or a senior executive. For good reasons too: your performance affects everyone in the company. Remember the last time you had a new CEO; how did everyone react for the first few weeks? It was likely endless commentary and observations about the strategic calls they made, the team they hired, decisions they put in place, promotions they gave, and what precisely they said in each meeting, press event, or corridor conversation. For a more in-depth set of Words That Work for launching into a new company or role, jump to Chapter 10, but now let's discuss why setting the right bar for performance is so critical and what to do about it.

The Control Fallacy

Despite what you might believe or tell yourself, your company performance is far more within your control than you believe. Of course, you couldn't have predicted a mistake by your competitor that opened up a new market opportunity for you, just as you perhaps couldn't have predicted a legislative change that resulted in unexpected costs, but you do control how you react to those unexpected changes. No leader could have predicted the global pandemic and its subsequent economic impact, but CEOs and boards around the world controlled how they reacted—and that differentiated performance. You set the tone. You set the expectations. You set the reality of your business performance. Your behavior is contagious. What you expect is what you get.

The Anita Effect

Here is the question asked in every debrief session at Amazon before an offer is extended to a candidate:

> **"**Is this person better than
> 50 percent of our people doing this job today?**"**

It is a thought-provoking question that encourages everyone to keep raising performance expectations while also making sure that you aren't settling for a rapid hire or waiting for the perfect hire. This is a fantastic way to raise the capability of your company with your new hires, but you must also make sure your existing teams are keeping up with the pace.

I was discussing the mediocre performance of a long-serving executive with a CEO client when I asked the question that I ask a variation of in every performance discussion:

> **"**What difference would
> it make if they performed as well as Anita?**"**

In this case, I already knew that Anita was her top-performing executive, and I needed her to visualize multiple Anitas on her executive team to see the possible impact of investing time in managing the performance of someone not meeting the mark. Immediately she jumped up to the whiteboard and drew a chart of the issues that could be solved if the underperforming leader could produce output similar to Anita's. It is easy to get into a rut and slowly lower your expectations, stop pointing out repetitive errors, and hold back on giving feedback because your past efforts haven't yielded results. Instead you have to intentionally reflect on how you and your company are creating Remarkable Performance.

The Right Height for Your Expectations

Think for a moment about someone remarkable who has worked for you in the past. Remind yourself what projects they worked on, which customers they supported, how their team performed, and what your financial results were when you worked together. Now complete the Remarkable Impact Reflection.

TABLE 2.1   Remarkable Impact Reflection

NAME:

1.   What was unique about their performance?
2.   What business impact did they have?
3.   How did that make your job more impactful and easier?
4.   What set them apart in their knowledge, skills and behaviors?
5.   How did their performance impact their peers?

As you complete the Remarkable Impact Reflection, you will notice that it allows you to uncover the impact their success has on not only the company's performance but also on their peers. When I speak at conferences on accelerating growth, one of my most popular sound-bites is always this one:

"Performance is contagious,
for better or for worse, and you get to decide.**"**

Just like I suggested considering the "Anita Effect" with the CEO I was working with, you can imagine your remarkable performer in every role on your team. That is the fuel you need to drive you through the necessary conversations to help them improve, adjust, or be replaced.

As CEO, you may be reflecting on which of your functions or divisions have set the right height for their performance expectations. Or perhaps you are a divisional executive or responsible for a function that you believe to be delivering remarkable performance yet aren't quite convinced that your peers are doing the same. This is where the Remarkable Performance Assessment (Figure 2.1) gives you a mechanism for evaluating the seven essential elements to create remarkable performance.

Remarkable Performance Assessment

1 Strategic clarity: We know where we are going and the speed and sequence of moves to get us there.

2 Aligned objectives: We create, monitor, and evaluate objectives across functions, regions, and teams.

3 Meaningful metrics: We have a shared understanding of the metrics that matter.

4 Clear leadership expectations: We describe specific expectations for managers at all levels.

5 Swift supportive action: When expectations are missed, rapid, specific feedback and support is given.

6 Mismatched employees: When a role outgrows a person, expectations change, or feedback doesn't work, we help people leave swiftly and with grace.

7 Careful rewards: Our rewards are clearly linked to individual and company performance, and personal behaviors.

Now that you know your most remarkable employees and the evaluation of the seven elements to create remarkable performance, you can follow the four phases to find the right Words That Work to make it happen:

Phase One: Setting Standards

Phase Two: Resetting Standards

FIGURE 2.1   Remarkable Performance Assessment

1.	Strategic clarity	/10
2.	Aligned objectives	/10
3.	Meaningful metrics	/10
4.	Clear leadership expectations	/10
5.	Swift supportive action	/10
6.	Managed mismatched employees	/10
7.	Careful rewards	/10

Rate each essential element out of 10

Phase Three: Support or Change

Phase Four: Action

While each stage is essential, the biggest oversight executives make is to start at Phase Three, thinking that you have already completed the first two phases sufficiently, when actually a rapid recap of how you set and reset expectations can resolve issues.

Phase One: Setting Standards

If your **Strategic Clarity** is strong from your Remarkable Performance Assessment in Figure 2.1, this makes it easier. Or you might have to ask:

"Do we all know where we are going and how we will get there?**"**

This question alone is often the center of my work with CEOs and executive teams. During my corporate career at Xbox, shortly after Nintendo launched the Wii games console where you could play virtual tennis with a plastic stick attached to the console with a wire, Xbox created an overall strategy to broaden its own appeal, to compete with Nintendo's Wii and Sony's PlayStation. Historically Xbox created racing and shooting games, but that overall calling was needed to make sure everyone had a shared understanding of where we were going. (Quite frankly, at the time that had varying degrees of success depending on which games studio you worked in.)

Once you are clear on your strategy, you then need to create **Aligned Objectives.**

"Do you have written objectives linked to the company strategy?**"**

That is a great question for evaluating how well the standards are set for you and your team. You can ask this for yourself and for the team that you manage. This is particularly helpful if you've recently had a new boss or have just joined the team, or when there hasn't been the discipline to set objectives and cascade them. Therefore, it is essential to spend time here and review the objectives for each member of your team, and their teams.

Phase Two: Resetting Standards

You may need to enter Phase Two if your business has significantly changed due to market conditions, a change of ownership, a new CEO, new product lines, or because you need to adjust because the output of an individual or team isn't meeting expectations and adjustments need to be made.

Phase Three: Support or Change

If you have set and reset expectations and are still not seeing the results you need, it is time to determine how you can best support the member of your team.

To effectively see change here you must deconstruct why you are seeing a performance gap and the root cause of that gap. Use the Mind the Performance Gap in Figure 2.2 to identify where your team member has gaps to close.

FIGURE 2.2   Mind the Performance Gap

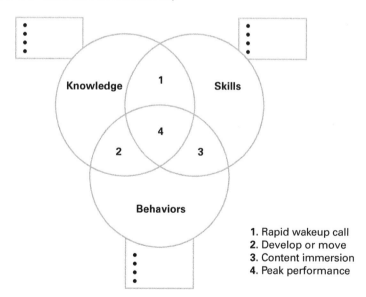

1. Rapid wakeup call
2. Develop or move
3. Content immersion
4. Peak performance

1   **The right knowledge and skills but gaps exist in required behaviors.** This needs a tough conversation on the specifics you want to change. This will either produce a rapid wake-up call and successful changes or may require specific real-time coaching and feedback.

2   **The gap is with skills, but knowledge and right behaviors are demonstrated.** Depending on the skills required, this could be solved by shadowing an expert, having a specific coach with experience in building those skills, or attending a learning experience where those skills are developed.

3   **Gap in knowledge, but the right skills and behaviors are demonstrated.** This could be addressed by attending topic-specific events, being mentored by an expert with the knowledge, or being given a stretch assignment.

As you manage this perceived or real performance gap, it is important to review what you are incentivizing. As I was writing this chapter, a divisional president called me asking for my help with an inconsistency in performance across his global teams. At the end of our conversation, I explained to him he didn't need my help, because his solution was simple: he just needed to change the incentive program for his global teams to reward the right results. Their compensation plans were not carefully created; they solely focused on top-line company results without accounting for profitable growth or regional success and failure.

No one will try to outperform if you spread your rewards across everyone like peanut butter on bread and fail to differentiate based on effort and impact. I'd only just moved to the United States with Microsoft when I learned the phrase "peanut buttering"—it was actually used in business meetings! As a British person recently relocated to Microsoft's headquarters in Seattle, I wondered exactly what this phrase meant. I quickly learned that it was shorthand for describing the effect of spreading a precious commodity across so many people that it lost its impact, just like if you spread too little peanut butter on too much bread, you lose the taste. Not that I am a fan of peanut butter, but the analogy stuck with me, and it is a rapid way to test just how you differentiate rewards based on performance.

Phase Four: Action

It is difficult for people to manage their team's performance if the best aren't being recognized or the worst aren't being dealt with by those above them. That is why swift action is essential. When the first three phases go well, this step is often forgotten, which is unfortunate because it can be a powerful learning experience. When your previous work to address performance gaps is resolved, take time to pause and validate the moment. Notice what has changed, how you identified and addressed it, and the results you saw. This is the perfect topic to include in one of your executive leadership speeches, because it is the best way to learn—from other leaders who have had a challenge leading their team that they resolved. Too often, these situations are forgotten about, not spoken about, or kept quiet, when in fact they should be used as learning moments for everyone to appreciate.

If the first three phases do not go well, then comes one of the most difficult types of conversations you have to have as an executive— letting someone know that they will no longer be able to continue in their role. Depending on the country you are doing business in, there are a number of potential chapters of advice that I could insert here, but these are not the type of details we are addressing. Instead, we are looking at what is relevant and applicable globally regarding the words to use in a discussion about the fact that it is not working out and alternative paths must be explored. That is the language you will learn here, and it is language that has worked for executives around the world.

The Art of Giving Feedback That Actually Changes Something

The number one piece of advice for giving feedback is not actually in the words you use; it is what happens immediately before you give feedback.

Welltory is one of many fitness apps that monitor your vital signs and analyze your stress levels and overall health. By scanning your finger with the camera and flash on your phone, it gives you a stress score, a productivity score, and an energy levels score. While you don't necessarily need a fancy watch or app to check your heart rate before a difficult conversation, it does help to mentally scan your physical and emotional state of mind. If you can check your emotions before you speak, you can make sure your message doesn't get lost by the way you deliver it.

In Chapter 7 we cover in depth one of the most difficult emotions— anger. You will learn how to understand your anger, and even learn to love it, but this preparation covers all of your emotions. Whether you are feeling frustrated, disappointed, annoyed, sad, scared, nervous, or angry, you have to shake that off before giving difficult feedback. Otherwise, your emotions will be a distraction and your message won't come across as clearly as it will if you are calm. Here is a critical question for those missing their performance goals:

"What do you think is holding back your ability to deliver?"

Overload, Mismatched, Disorganized, Disengaged, or Distracted

When an executive is not performing, you must pause to ask why, first by asking for some self-reflection. After that, you may have to do further digging to really uncover what is happening. After three decades of working with leaders around the globe, I have found that it is usually one of five things that hold back an individual's ability to deliver:

1 **Overloaded.** The person is not delegating effectively, or lacks enough of the right talent to delegate to.

2 **Mismatched.** The person lacks the skills or been-there-done-that experience to know what to do and how to do it.

3 **Disorganized.** The person is unable to manage their own or their team's time.

4 **Disengaged.** The person has lost the passion and excitement to inspire themselves and their team.

5 **Distracted.** Something else in their life is distracting them from peak performance.

Even the most successful executives can take on too much, or have a capacity issue in their team. Your job is to uncover it, confront it, and support how you can address it.

Tracking Performance Progress

By now you have evaluated your team and noted words you can use, but this is where feelings of being overwhelmed and frustrated can kick in. I will often hear an executive say:

> **"**What is it going to take
> for my team to proactively follow up and deliver?**"**

And that is precisely what I then tell them they need to ask their team! Sometimes it can feel like you are repeating the same annoying announcements you hear at an airport, and it can sometimes feel like your team is tuning out your requests—just as easily as you tune out the familiar requests to not leave your bags unattended. While you are teaching your team new habits, there are two simple but powerful tools they can use. I share these regularly with my clients: the Weekly Progress Report and the Executive Leadership Team Summary.

The first is a simple format for receiving a weekly update at a set time and day each week from individuals on your team. Here is what it contains:

WEEKLY PROGRESS REPORT

Completed

- Projects and initiatives delivered

In Progress

- Projects/initiatives/work in progress where you can highlight status and any change in expected time of completion

---

In Planning

- Projects/initiatives/work that has not yet started but you are planning, or things you are hearing might need input from you or your team

Questions for Me

- Here you add what you need from me at a high level, roadblocks, and escalations (e.g., can you decide on X, by Y date?)
- Can you give me any feedback on my involvement in the executive staff meeting?
- I need thirty minutes with you before Wednesday to review the board presentation

This allows you to have a regular predictable update in a concise format giving you a snapshot of where your team is meeting, missing, or exceeding your expectations.

The second tool that CEOs love to use is the Executive Leadership Team Summary (Figure 2.3), a recap of your executive team, tracking current deliverables, gaps, your actions, and next steps. I use this tool with many of the executives I work with as it allows them to give me a rapid recap so I can easily provide insights and advice.

Have you ever sat in an important conversation and had your thoughts take over—perhaps wondering what your boss is writing in her notebook? Curious if you read that expression as a note of support or one of confusion? Or do you reflect on a conversation wishing you had stopped to make sure your point was fully understood?

When giving feedback to increase performance, crystal clear communication is the greatest unlock. It's critical to be able to clearly connect what we say, what we mean, what is heard, and what others remember to our true intentions. Figure 2.4 shows that what you say isn't always what you were thinking, and if you forget to state your true intentions, it is easy to get crossed wires. Chapter 4 dives into creating internal communication mechanisms that allow you to get your message across.

FIGURE 2.3 Executive Leadership Team Summary

Leader	Goals Agreed?	Current Status	Current Asks	Gaps	Your Actions and Timing	Comments/ Questions
Name	*Yes/No*	*Current status of role and function*	*What specific goals / tasks / projects are underway?*	*Where are you seeing gaps in strategy, function, capability or capacity?*	*Requirements for you that are underway or you need to start*	*Observations, questions for me, areas to consider, general musings*

FIGURE 2.4   Crystal Clear Communication

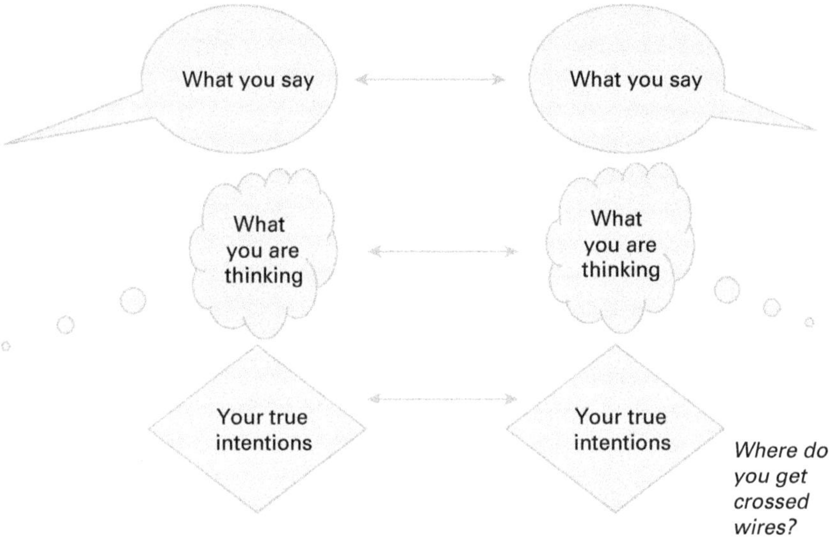

Countdown to Your Best Year Yet

As we wrap up this chapter, here's a simple rapid implementation tool for you. Answer this crucial question:

❝What would make the next twelve months your best year yet?❞

Imagine you could time travel ahead 365 days; see yourself there already. Now write down the 5, 4, 3, 2, 1 countdown, and answer the following:

---

5 Objectives You Will Have Achieved

These can be in your whole life, not just your work life, and they don't have to all be about revenue, financial metrics, and market share.

4 Metrics So You Will Know You Have Succeeded

What indicators will show you have achieved your objectives?

---

3 Reasons Why It Matters to You

Answer my favorite question: So what? Why do you care if you achieve this or not?

2 Mindset Changes Needed to Make It Happen

How do you need to get out of your own way, or what new beliefs do you need to hold on to?

1 Piece of Advice You Need Now

What advice do you need so that you can get there joyfully? I deliberately state joyfully, because many achieve incredible things, but most are not doing it in a joyful way. It's hard work, and it seems to be too much of a hard slog.

When I complete this exercise with leaders in keynotes, workshops, or one-on-one, I have a two-minute sand timer in my hand that I flip over for a rapid first pass.

Julie Simpson, CEO and Founder of ResourceiT Consulting Ltd. in Europe, completed this exercise on an executive leadership forum that I run:

> I realized I needed to put more focus on what success looks like for myself. As senior leaders, we're all really good at doing that for other people but don't necessarily take the time to do it for ourselves. I do think it's about the mirror that we are holding up to ourselves. We've got where we are because we're successful, hardworking, intelligent executives who are influential, and we are great leaders. We are very good at what we do and we're where we are because of that, and we don't necessarily push down enough.

A week later, Simpson called me and shared that she had taken steps toward the objectives she had laid out, and already felt freer and more in control:

> Following on from the conversation we had last week about holding a mirror up, I think my biggest failing is that I consistently take up the slack and that holds me back. My one piece of advice would be taking

your own medicine and not feeling like you're the answer to every problem or deficiency within the business. I have realized that I need to get back to delegation and prioritization.

Another leader, Dr. Renee V. Pizarro, HPE NA Commercial Segment Sales Director, who completed the 5, 4, 3, 2, 1 countdown viewed success in broader terms than business metrics and impact:

A defining moment for me in my career was when I stepped back and I redefined success. It wasn't about checking off the list or this great presentation or that I won a new customer. It was about how I create exponential success for the organization. I became engaged in more forums as a Hispanic female in technology. My objective is how I can advance and open doors for other Hispanic females in technology. How do I use my position of influence to impact others so I can define impact beyond my own success? My lasting legacy would be how many other people I could help by advancing their legacies or their own success. A driving force for this shift was when my mom was diagnosed with pancreatic cancer and that jolted me into a place where I had no choice as her primary caregiver, and I needed to do that at work and at home. I had to feel okay with hiring someone who would come into my home to clean and cook every single day because I didn't have time for that anymore. I needed to spend time caring for my mother.

The final activity for you to consider in this chapter is one where you reset where you spend your time and energy. You have new words to use to set and maintain your high-performance bar, and you have new ways to review your leadership team and manage your team's individual and collective outputs. At this point the most successful executives take a gargantuan leap in productivity because they know exactly how to prioritize their time. As you rise through your various promotions, you have to shed the desire to do and the desire to take on more activity. You need to replace old habits with new ones and keep pressing reset to make mental shifts and calibrate your actual time spent.

It's what I call focusing on the right spot and time spent in various time frames: zero to thirty days, three to six months, one year out. Where are you spending your time on that continuum? Then how much of it is execution versus planning versus big blue sky thinking? If that was on an axis and you were to draw a circle of where you want to be versus where you are today, you could see the gap that you have to try to close. We explore this further in Chapter 11.

Here's your last reflection for this chapter. Take a pad of paper and create three columns. In column one, list what you do today that you want to keep doing. Then you jump to the far side with column three, which is things you do today that you should not be doing and someone else needs to be doing. In the middle column put the question mark items, such as I don't know whether I should be doing this, or who I should give it to. Using the lens of how you can achieve your 5, 4, 3, 2, 1 countdown, consider where you should be spending your time and energy right now and what you need to delegate.

This might give you a reality check about what to move off your plate and how you might be able to free up more time. In the next chapter we will explore the right words that work to get others to cooperate with you.

Rapid Remarkable Performance Words That Work

Preparation for Feedback

"I am curious to understand...**"**

"Can you see this from a different point of view?**"**

"It is important to me that I hear your candid reaction...**"**

"Tell me about your view on...**"**

Power of Self-Evaluation

"Share how you would evaluate your success in this project...**"**

"Which functions would
rate this a success or suggest room for improvement?**"**

Probing

"I'd love to hear your reaction...**"**

"Tell me about your view on...**"**

"What would you say if you were being really candid?**"**

"Tell me something that you don't think I'd be aware of...**"**

"What else can you tell me about...**"**

"I would love more examples...**"**

Missed Expectations

"I am concerned you are missing your agreed commitments...**"**

"It is crucial that you are
able to __, and I'm not consistently seeing that.**"**

"Is there anything else
that I should be aware of that is causing this?**"**

"What do you think is a realistic plan to get back on track?**"**

"What support do you need
from me to catch up before quarter end?**"**

Bonus offer: If you would like an electronic version of the Remarkable
Impact Reflection along with all of the other tools in this book, visit
www.wrightwordsthatwork.com.

03

Getting Others to Cooperate

CEOs cannot simply sit in a cave talking and listening to their own echo. Nor can they fail to speak their thoughts. They must influence others, drive cooperation, and make change happen at a significant scale. This chapter explores how to understand how much cooperation a CEO or executive can achieve. Once you understand your Executive Power Circle, you can follow the steps in this chapter to increase your impact. You will also learn simple ways to test and build cooperation from others as well as the secrets to leading change at scale with tools that help you communicate, evaluate, and implement change that will affect your profit, revenue, and market share.

CHAPTER TOPICS

- Why We Pre-Worry Away Our Words
- Knowing Where People Are Starting From
- How to Give and Receive Support
- Five Cooperation Foundations
- Your Executive Power Circle
- The Perfect One-on-One Conversation
- Words That Don't Work

Why We Pre-Worry Away Our Words

Before we dive into this chapter on how to get others to cooperate, I will state the obvious important point often overlooked:

❝Words only work if you say them out loud.**❞**

In my thousands of interactions with leaders, I hear more regret about what was not said than what was said. This excessive self-editing can cause you to freeze when it is exactly the time to speak up.

The number one cause for this pre-worry is self-doubt. While impostor syndrome has been well documented, what is rarely looked at is why those voices of doubt can freeze our ability to move forward. In my conversations with leaders around the world, I have found three key reasons for this self-doubt:

1 An incident from your past that shaped your default reactions.

2 A voice from your past whose volume is too loud in your head.

3 Unfounded fears of success or failure.

The caveat I always provide in my executive conversations is that I am not a trained therapist, but I do know the boundaries of my work and where speaking with a trained expert could be helpful. We don't have to be therapists to know that our past experiences shape our current mindset. Sometimes you need advice from different sources to reset your current thinking. I experienced this myself as I was writing this book. Before I sat down to write this chapter, I was riding my Peloton spin bike at home, and instructor Alex Toussaint screamed out this thought-jarring soundbite via the video screen:

❝You woke up today. You are blessed!**❞**

This was right after receiving a text telling me a fellow mother of three from my daughters' school was in the ICU in critical condition: Alex's words really worked for me on this day. I was getting my pre-morning workout in and preparing myself for writing this book and the next virtual workshop for a technology company on rapidly growing their sales. The workshop includes helping sales teams get in and out of their own heads at the right time, showing the value of using others to help deconstruct what is going on in your head. I saw from Alex's social media feed that he was appearing on the US talk show *Today* later that day. On the show, host Carson Daly shared his struggles with mental health and how the value of Alex and his bike rides goes beyond the sweat and leaderboard status Peloton is famous for. Maybe your version of Alex Toussaint is your therapist, maybe it's your meditation or your yoga class, but finding a way to talk more to those close to you about what's going on inside your head will improve your mental and physical strength.

I have learned that many leaders find value in Toussaint and other Peloton instructors; they share messages that speak to your heart, use uplifting real-talk, and play brilliant music right when you need it. As you prepare for getting others to cooperate in new ways, there's another Toussaint quote from one of his Peloton rides that you may want to ask others when you are seeking their cooperation:

❝Physically you might be ok. But internally are you really ok?**❞**

Knowing Where People Are Starting From

Have you ever been frustrated that someone wasn't willing to cooperate? Or felt that what you thought was a perfectly simple or reasonable request didn't seem to be that reasonable or clear to someone else?

One of the greatest mistakes you can make in trying to get people to cooperate is failing to be empathetic. You simply cannot assume that they are in the same space you are. It is easy to skip over this step and jump straight to tactics and tools to get anyone to cooperate with you when in fact you need to pause and pay attention to where the person you want to influence currently is. This could be empathy towards a frustrating last meeting someone attended or a more significant challenge in someone's work or whole life.

Never was this more noticeable than in the 2020 global coronavirus pandemic. Businesses, families, and individuals all reacted to the pandemic in different ways. Influencing during a crisis requires an elevated level of focus and attention. In the Wright house our lead-up to the pandemic started one morning in December 2019; I was carefully walking down our creaky basement steps to tackle our never-ending pile of laundry when I discovered murky water covering the bottom few steps. My three daughters like to remind me of what I said when I discovered this disaster, and it certainly falls into the words that DON'T work category! This curse-inducing flood led to us rapidly moving house. We found, moved, and unpacked right before the pandemic took over. We adjusted to life with five of us in a house, two of us working, while attempting to be the best substitute teachers we could be to our then twelve-year-old and two ten-year-old daughters.

Like many others who were not frontline workers, I rapidly shifted my business to working virtually after quickly converting our attic storage room into my temporary office. I predict that there will be many in-depth studies on the effects of the Covid-19 pandemic, and not just on the obvious points of fast-tracked technology implementation, the shift to online shopping, and accelerated remote working, but more significantly on the effect on social dynamics—the deeper impact of how we interact, communicate, influence, persuade, and work together.

When a major change or unexpected situation arises, there are ten perfect words to use:

"How does this impact you and how can I help?**"**

This will help you understand where people are and be empathetic to their situation. It will allow you to reflect and ask yourself, how are different people experiencing this situation right now? Your experience is not universally felt, yet too often we make that assumption. The most important step is to ask and listen. Businesses that ask their customers this question during unexpected times are more successful, and in Chapter 5 we will explore some examples of this.

How to Give and Receive Support

"My hand is on your back.**"**

That has to be the most powerful phrase I read during the pandemic, and I didn't read it in a leadership book or hear it from a management guru from Harvard. I heard this phrase on a social media group connected to the Peloton bike instructor Cody Rigsby; his fans, called #boocrew, have a unique vibe of empathy, support, positivity, and zero drama.

The phrase brought tears to my eyes every time I read it. It was originally said after someone shared a difficulty they were experiencing, some trauma or unexpected misfortune. The idea of having someone's hand on your back reminded me of teaching my three daughters to ride their bikes. I'd run alongside them as they wobbled along the path in the park, and every so often I would put my hand on their back to steady them, reassure them, and build their confidence. The following week I was hosting an executive forum group with twelve executives from technology companies, and during the call one of the executives shared challenging situations, having dealt with an unexpected merger whilst managing some tough personal health news. Three other executives followed with different but similar stories of both work and personal upheavals, some positive, some difficult. At the end of our call I shared my discovery of this new phrase, and then I addressed each of them in turn, letting them know,

"Trevor, my hand is on your back.**"**

"Allison, my hand is on your back.**"**

"Derek, my hand is on your back.**"**

A very powerful way to end a group conversation, and all from lessons from a members group supporting a spin cycle instructor!

How often have you had that level of support at work? Can you imagine having an environment like that? Reflecting on what I read on this social media group and how any leader could translate it into their work life reminded me of the power of community and the need for a set of shared values. That is the way you influence others to create a safe space for others to be vulnerable, truth-telling, and supportive of each other. To achieve that, you must first understand what elements make a strong foundation for cooperation.

Five Cooperation Foundations

It's easy to notice when cooperation is failing, but can you describe precisely what it takes to create an environment where cooperation comes naturally? I developed the Five Cooperation Foundations (Figure 3.1) as conversation starters for teams and companies that want to increase their cross-team results. When a board chair of a technology company asked me if I could meet with a CEO and his executive team because they weren't delivering their quarterly earnings results as expected, he shared his concern that each member of the executive team seemed to be operating on their own, and that their strategy and implementation lacked cohesiveness. When I met with each of them, I asked them to score the Five Cooperation Foundations using the following scoring system: Green—it is a consistent strength; Yellow—there is room for improvement or greater consistency; and Red—it is a concern that needs dedicated attention.

The five foundations are:

1 I feel confident everyone has my back.

2 I observe that across teams, functions, and locations, we are all working to common goals.

3 I have experienced that asking for help is acceptable and encouraged.

4 I have been part of successes that are jointly celebrated.

5 I have seen mistakes objectively deconstructed for lessons learned, not to attribute blame.

FIGURE 3.1   Five Cooperation Foundations

I feel like everyone
has my back

Across team, function, location we
are all pulling in the same direction

Asking for help is
acceptable + encouraged

Successes are
jointly celebrated

Mistakes are objectively deconstructed for
lessons learned, not the blame game

Rating
Green: Consistent strength
Yellow: Room for improvement
Red: Concern needing dedicated attention

As they individually shared their color coding and answered what it would take to make each foundation a strength, there was a common reaction from all eight executives: they realized they had never had the conversation about how they worked together or how they wanted cooperation to occur in their company. Without me needing to tell the Pause Game: Play Game story described in Chapter 1, they had discovered for themselves the power of taking time out to intentionally declare expectations of how they would communicate and cooperate. We dedicated time to continue the collective discussion in the strategy retreat we had planned for the following week. Figure 3.2 shares how each leader scored with this Five Cooperation Foundations Team Sample.

As you look at the scores in Figure 3.2, reflect on:

– What observations do you have?

– How do you think the outliers experience the team?

– If you were the CEO of this team, what new expectations would you set?

FIGURE 3.2   Five Cooperation Foundations – scoring

Green	**I feel like everyone has my back**
Yellow	**Across team, function, location we are all pulling in the same direction**
Red	**Asking for help is acceptable + encouraged**
Yellow	**Successes are jointly celebrated**
Red	**Mistakes are objectively deconstructed for lessons learned, not the blame game**

Rating

Green: Consistent strength
Yellow: Room for improvement
Red: Concern needing dedicated attention

Having Your Back Put to the Test

Maya Dukes had been in her new role as creative director for less than four weeks. It was her first major presentation and she had diligently prepared for it. Ten minutes prior to walking in the door of the meeting room, the president replied to her pre-read with stomach-churning feedback: "This is not how I see this at all. You have not fully understood this, and I disagree with you." Ever had a similar somersault-inducing moment? Fortunately for Maya, as she walked down the hallway her manager met with her and said the most powerful phrase:

> **"I've got your back."**

That was all Maya needed to hear, those four powerful, supportive words. Indeed, her manager did have her back. At the start of the meeting Maya's manager kicked off the conversation by saying,

> **"I think there was some confusion in our objectives here..."**

In doing so, she immediately defused the situation and allowed everyone to create a shared understanding of exactly what they hoped to accomplish. What could have been a disastrous first meeting with the president turned into a perfectly positioned meeting, all because Maya's manager of only four weeks clearly demonstrated she had her hand on Maya's back as she took her first critical meeting.

The key to Maya's success was her intentional executive launch that she had prepared for earlier that month, which is further explored in Chapter 10. You must consider who is supporting you, who you need to influence, and how strong your Power Circle is.

Your Executive Power Circle

I have been studying *The Wall Street Journal* weekend feature "My Board" for the last year and my theory rings true. CEOs generally surround themselves with people who are like them. The feature highlights a prominent CEO and shares the top five advisors that they have in their personal board of advisors. What I observed from reading the column for the last year is that there is a reason why the boys' club is a much-used phrase, because when you talk about CEOs influencing CEOs, they are indeed predominately male. In fact, if you need convincing further, there are more CEOs called David in the NASDAQ than there are women CEOs.[1] The more senior the role, the more I have observed executives wanting to hire people they have worked with in the past or who have a strong referral from their personal network. So how exactly do we break the cycle? You need to shatter your own circle and find ways to break into new circles, elevate the people you hang out with, and, most importantly, use the right words to influence others.

One of the most common stumbling blocks to working on your personal advisory board, or as I like to call it your Executive Power Circle (Figure 3.3), is that you will be in one of two places: very focused on the here and now of a current project you are trying to launch, or contemplating your future and wanting to invest in building your network to prepare for a pending change. It is why I show two halves of your Power Circle—one focused on today, and the other on the future.

You can fail epically to have others cooperate with you if you don't have the right executive support, cross-functional cooperation, or backing of your CFO. So many brilliant ideas get buried in companies due to a lack of executive support. The very best companies are taking their innovation sandbox ideas and rapidly accelerating them through the company. But that only works if you've got executive support. When I work with chief innovation officers or executives in charge of innovation labs, I explain the importance of this mapping using five simple steps:

1 Consider your current objectives and priorities and complete who you need to have cooperating with you to succeed today, whether they are on your team, functional leaders, senior leaders, or external to your organization. Include everyone you need.

2 Given your future aspirations, now consider who needs to be on the right-hand side of the circle.

3 Now using the thumbs up, thumbs down, and question mark coding, evaluate how well each of those in your Power Circle cooperates with you today.

4 Add in the advisors you have mentoring, coaching, or guiding you.

5 Note the fuel to the Power Circle and consider what you may focus on first to strengthen your circle.

Your Executive Power Circle will accelerate or decelerate your success depending on how well you attend to it. Getting others to cooperate involves you having a well-connected Power Circle, which I describe as a hydrated set of connections.

I was being interviewed by Rachel Pasqua, formerly the CMO of women's executive network mBolden, for their podcast, when I was reminded of a keynote talk she had heard me give. On stage, I had shared what seems to be an easy task but in reality is tough to prioritize. I asked the audience: "Stop and consider: is your network dehydrated?" Pasqua shared how she could see this look of sheer

FIGURE 3.3   Executive Power Circle

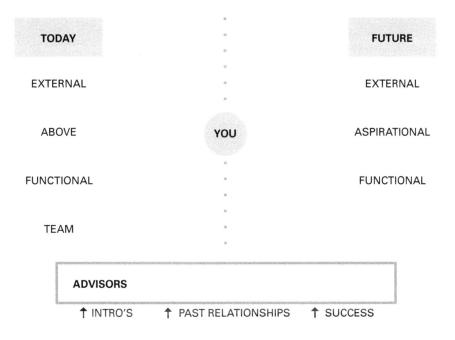

terror across almost all faces in the room. Theoretically it should be the easiest activity—to nurture human connections who can support you, elevate you, and help you get to the next level. Yet more often than not, daily priorities take over. If you would like an added push to prioritize this now, understand that you have a six-month lead and lag time on the attention you pay to your connections. If you ignore them, it will be six months before it impacts you; similarly, if you want to start reconnecting, expect six months before you are back to peak levels of connection, responsiveness, and support. With that in mind, who could you call today to start reconnecting? Once they respond, set up time to talk; this is the next opportunity to create meaningful interactions that can allow you to encourage others to cooperate, but to do that you need to know how to have the perfect one-on-one conversation.

The Perfect One-on-One Conversation

One question provides a powerful start to any one-on-one conversation. It allows you to quickly clarify what you want to achieve and give the other person a chance to reprioritize:

> **"**I have three topics: a, b, and
> c—is there anything else you want to cover?**"**

It might seem a little direct for some, but I guarantee you that those you meet with will be eternally grateful for intentional focus in your time together.

During my corporate career at Microsoft, I never met the team that designed the reoccurring meeting feature in Outlook, but that seemingly innocent feature is one of the greatest time thieves across companies around the world. To combat the ill-thought-through reoccurring meetings in every single one of your next one-on-ones, ask this important question:

> **"**What is the right frequency at which we should be meeting right now?**"**

Simply asking the question will cause you both to pause and be intentional with how you spend your time together. The cadence doesn't have to be the same each season. Depending on the fluctuations of your business, your frequency of meeting should also change. How many hours of time can you give back to yourself and free up for your team right now?

> **"**Sow the seed, water the seed, walk away, return and harvest the seed.**"**

That is one of the most concise and memorable descriptions of how to influence others I have heard. It came from Curt Kroll, Senior Director, Sierra Constellation Partners. I had observed it for myself as we worked together at a private equity-backed company creating their five-year strategy. The most powerful part that many executives miss is knowing when to walk away and when to return again. That intentional persistence will strengthen your influence strategies, as long as you don't use any of the following words.

Words That Don't Work

Before we conclude this chapter, I want to pause and share some reverse advice, which means what not to do, or *Words That Don't Work* when encouraging others to cooperate with you:

Don't say this	Say this instead
"You just don't understand."	
Rather than putting the focus on their lack of understanding, consider that you might not be explaining it well enough. Instead say:	
	"I didn't do a good job of explaining..."
"I've already got the CEO's approval."	
Try to get support and cooperation because it is the right thing for the business, not because the CEO said so:	
	"Let me explain the value and impact of this idea..."
"You are the only one who disagrees with me."	
Instead of singling someone out for their different opinion, get curious as to why they have an alternative point of view. Try this:	
	"That's a unique perspective, explain more..."
"I need you to..."	
Before you demand from others, ask what you can do to help them:	
	"What do you need from me?"
"I am fine, how are you?"	
Lead with vulnerability, and share what you need and why.	
	"I'm having a tough time figuring out how to..."

(continued)

(continued)

Don't say this	Say this instead
"Can I ask a favor on this…"	
	Asking for advice increases the probability someone will respond, and say yes:
	"I would love to ask for your advice on…"
"This has gone wrong and I need your team to help fix…"	
	When you need cooperation after a failure, admit it and take ownership:
	"I made a mistake and I'd appreciate your help to resolve it…"
"Your team needs to support this launch…"	
	Be candid about the upsides and downsides of a project:
	"This project is not without risk, I'd love your advice on mitigation on…"

Endnote

1 Johnson, S, Hekman, D and Chan, E (2016) If there's only one woman in your candidate pool, there's statistically no chance she'll be hired, *Harvard Business Review*, https://hbr.org/2016/04/if-theres-only-one-woman-in-your-candidate-pool-theres-statistically-no-chance-shell-be-hired (archived at https://perma.cc/726M-4CD4)

04

Creative Internal Communications

Knowing who you are and letting others see the full multifaceted version of you is essential for effectively communicating your purpose, profit, and performance. The world of business dramatically evolved in 2020 as the Covid-19 pandemic forced companies to permit their employees to work from home and learn new ways to communicate and lead through a black rectangular screen. This historic time in corporate history forced many to switch their communications from meeting in conference room B to Zoom call meeting ID 536-6732 rather than getting creative about how to inspire and inform their employees.

Ambivalence is the greatest thief of productivity. Creative communication methods can combat ambivalence and accelerate performance. This chapter provides readers with an evaluation to test their current ability to communicate creatively, along with a practical guide to improve personal skills and company communication mechanisms.

CHAPTER TOPICS

- Your Purpose Pyramid
- The Power of Music
- The Change Tornado
- The Role of the Chief of Staff

At the heart of all powerful communications is the beat of a great story well told. If you want to share your story, often you have to ask others for their story first. This brings me to the most powerful first question you can ask someone when you want to get to know them better.

"Tell me your story.**"**

Not only is this a powerful interview question when hiring, it is also an essential communication tool for getting to know those around you.

To succeed in communicating internally, you must build connections with those around you. I'll never forget the feedback I heard after walking into a new role with a European team in which I was to complete a thirty-day listening tour. I was visiting all the subsidiaries across six different European countries to understand how the company was performing after a series of acquisitions. As we discussed the product plans, sales results, and profit projections, the most common commentary I heard was that nobody really knew who their new president was, even though he had visited and sent regular company updates via email since joining the year prior. This president was not alone in skipping over a more in-depth introduction, because it is easy to wallow in financials, metrics, board preparation, and investor briefings. There's a reason for that: the alternative requires you to be more vulnerable, transparent, and talk at a depth you may never have before. If you haven't already skipped on to the next chapter because of the awkwardness of what you can predict will come next, stay with me and I will provide the tools that have successfully helped leaders unlock a new level of communication and connection with employees, customers, and stakeholders.

The following month I was traveling with the European president, let's call him Derek to protect his identity, and I had time to ask some questions. Many great conversations happen in airports while waiting to board a flight, and after hearing about Derek's background, I knew his teams would devour his story if they had a chance to hear it.

Your Purpose Pyramid

After a couple of decades honing these questions with hundreds of leaders in various industries around the world, I created the Purpose Pyramid to allow anyone to reflect on their background and stories. Figure 4.1 summarizes this approach. The seven layers of the Purpose Pyramid allow you to extract and build your personal story, which will become the foundation of your internal corporate communication explored in this chapter, and will feed into your external communications strategy with Wall Street or the City and the media, which is covered in Chapter 9.

Let's start with the first layer: defining experiences. Does everyone know who you are? It is common for those you have worked with for many years to not know your history, your story, how you started out, who your most inspirational boss was, or what you learned while working as a teenager. Think of this like your foundation, your

FIGURE 4.1 Your Purpose Pyramid

defining moments, almost as though you were summarizing your life story for your biography, but in headline form, not detailed chapters. Knowing and sharing your story is crucial to your team knowing who you are, what is important to you as a leader, and how you got where you are today.

Do you remember the first seven jobs you had growing up? What did you learn from your summer jobs, part-time jobs, or volunteer work? That is usually an easy place to start because it is simple to remember, and you can often extract life lessons from each of those jobs. Next you're required to go a little deeper: what defining moments from your family life are you willing to share? I deliberately add the caveat of what you are willing to share, because I recognize that not everyone is ready to share just any story from their early years; simply consider which might be most relevant. You can even start at the surface level of where you were born, your heritage, who is in your family, who played an important role in your life growing up, your school or college life. This may be an area you come back to after starting at the surface factual level, or it may vary for different audiences. Here's an example so you get to know a little more about me.

My first seven jobs as a teenager and what I learned:

1 Newspaper deliverer
   Like Walt Disney himself, I got up at 6 am to deliver the morning newspapers before I went to school.
   My lesson: I learned the productivity hack of getting up before everyone else.

2 Babysitter
   Three rambunctious kids once locked me out of the house when I was a thirteen-year-old babysitting for the summer.
   My lesson: I learned great negotiating skills. (I seriously needed them to open the front door, fast!)

3 Lottery scratch card door-to-door sales
   Before the National Lottery existed in the UK, I sold scratch cards every Wednesday to a regular set of customers who agreed to allow me to knock on their door at a set time each week. It was like Amazon Prime before Jeff Bezos had even considered it.

My lesson: I learned that people will buy anything if you bring it to them regularly.

4 Ice cream sales

Restaurateur Brian Murdoch used to freshly make real ice cream out of four ingredients. I sold them along the river in the tourist town of Stourport-on-Severn in England.

My lesson: Simplicity works. Provide what your customer needs but might not know they need at precisely the right place.

5 Cafe caterer

British sports team Weston-super-Mare Football Club had a match day coffee shop where I worked with my sister and mum.

My lesson: Speed is essential. In a football (soccer) match, there is a fifteen-minute half-time break when everyone wants tea, coffee, and a burger. You must batch process and prepare to make the most money during that short profit-making window.

6 Lingerie sales

Jeanette Payton, the Lingerie Store manager of British retailer Secrets, taught me the art of selling at my Saturday job and was my inspiration for the start of my retail career.

My lesson: I learned that a few choices rather than endless choices increase the speed of customer decision-making.

7 Managing Director

I founded my first company when I was fifteen. Sponsored by HSBC, we had to raise money by issuing shares, choosing a product, developing a marketing strategy, and building and selling the products. It ended with writing an annual report and presenting our financial results and lessons learned to a panel of business leaders.

My lesson: Practical experience is more valuable than any exam or test.

What if you asked your team to share their first seven jobs and the lessons that they learned from them at your next team meeting or corporate event? Imagine if you had the rich examples and story starters like I provided above? These offer endless connection points and seeds sown for others to pick up on.

What did you learn about me from my list? That I'm British, that I have connections to football, that I worked in retail, that I founded a company as a teenager, and much more. These are what I call "story starters," starting threads of a story that can lead to connections, conversations, and mutual interest. You can ask your team after this exercise this one powerful question:

"What are your story starters?"

The second step in your Purpose Pyramid is declaring what values are important to you; I suggest you pick your top seven. If this is new to you, consider what your guiding principles are for how you work and live your life. Often, you must create your first set of values and then sit with them for a while as you work and spend time with friends and family. Then you will become more conscious of what you hold dear and what is important to you. You can also identify your values by working backward from a situation where your values conflicted with someone else's. This creates a values dilemma and tension, allowing you to see what is important about how you work.

The third step is stating your *raison d'être*, or your reason for being. This elevates above your job title, functional expertise, or any letters after your name. It's a description of your why, or your purpose.

The fourth layer to describe in your Purpose Pyramid is what those around you can expect from you—your personal commitment to your team, your peers, your boss, your board, your social circle, and your family. This then leads to you committing in the fifth layer to what you expect of others, noting your expectations or requests of others in how they communicate with you, involve you in decisions, and keep you informed. These two expectation-setting steps are often where friction and conflict can arise because of a failure to communicate up front about mutual expectations.

The penultimate step is very specific but valuable. It is how you want others to disagree with you. This is specifically called out because of the variety in personal preferences and the impact it can have on the results you create. Some leaders love public disagreement, whereas others vehemently oppose it, expecting it all to happen behind closed doors. Amazon is a company that expects debates and disagreements to be front of stage with nothing hidden behind the curtain, regardless of the relative seniority of those challenging and those being challenged. When I was part of the Fashion Leadership team in 2011, this became quite a stumbling block for many leaders who joined Amazon from other companies where a polite public performance of solidarity was expected and rewarded, then disagreements were worked out afterward one-to-one. This contrasted greatly with Amazon's norms of the scrappy "let's put all the issues and disagreements out on the table and hash them out bluntly and forcefully without holding back."

The final step at the top of the Purpose Pyramid is your soundbites, or catchphrases you use to display all the lower layers of the pyramid. I describe these as footprints in the sand: it is what remains when you have left and others can use those footprints to follow or to remember you were there. Just like actual footprints in the sand, they can be washed away so you have to keep repeating your soundbites and making more footprints for the soundbites that you want throughout your communications.

Now you have completed all seven steps of your Purpose Pyramid, you can refer to this in your communications and use the content in the messages you want to share, not just about your strategy and business results but about who you are as a leader and human being. It's your story that led you to where you are today.

That is how people get to know the real you, not the fake you. In Chapter 5 we will explore how to understand and strengthen your company Purpose Pyramid, but let's first take a musical break.

The Power of Music

One of my favorite songs is "Optimistic" by Sounds of Blackness. The lyrics are meaningful to me. I first listened to it when I was seventeen in England. My boyfriend had just unceremoniously ended our relationship with me two days before I had important exams and I was feeling really miserable. That song became my anthem while I was taking my exams. Ever since, whenever I've had a tough time or whenever I just needed some hope, I play it. It reminds me of my seventeen-year-old self struggling to take tests. Music isn't played enough at work. If you have joined me on any of my virtual events you will have seen how I use music throughout my sessions; contact me and I will invite you to the next event I am holding so you can experience it for yourself, as a gift from me.

When I used to visit my client Sonos, the speaker company, of course they had a DJ every week, with their speakers being tested and showcased throughout their Santa Barbara headquarters. But why is it the exception rather than the norm? There is a unique opportunity to uplift and connect with how you communicate through the power of music.

The 18-month window of remote working for so many around the world due to the Covid-19 pandemic meant a new way of working and living our lives. During that time, companies had people in different cities that were in lockdown, out of lockdown, all trying to figure out how to lead, sell, build relationships through this screen, while taking care of their whole lives. Music is a different way to connect with people because you can tell stories. I often make the first few minutes of a meeting a little more interesting by playing part of a tune, telling my story, and encouraging others to share their favorite song for a particular moment. I would ask,

"Tell me one of your inspirational songs that you listen to when…"

You can then have someone on the call create a playlist with the collection of people's favorite tracks that others can listen to; it memorializes the moment with your team and gives you some different ways to connect.

The Change Tornado

For internal communications to be successful, it has to incorporate how you lead others through change. For change to be successful, people have to understand and believe in the change. You may rarely get blind followers who are happy to take your word for it, but that is the exception. For everyone else you have to help them understand, then believe, why you want to make changes.

While the change curve describing how change affects you is well documented and extensively used, I describe change as more of a tornado than a curve, as shown in the Change Tornado in Figure 4.2. Change can be similar to a tornado. You start with the anticipation, the worry about what may come next. Then the tornado hits and there is often devastation and damage. Then you may have a freeze in the eye of the storm before more devastation and needing a rebuild phase to assess and repair the damage caused. Can you relate to that description for a recent change you experienced?

The Change Tornado is a great tool for understanding the multiple dimensions of change. In Figure 4.3, the Crucial Phases of Change, you can understand the required level of involvement of executives, managers, and teams for making changes effective, and the reality of

FIGURE 4.2   The Change Tornado

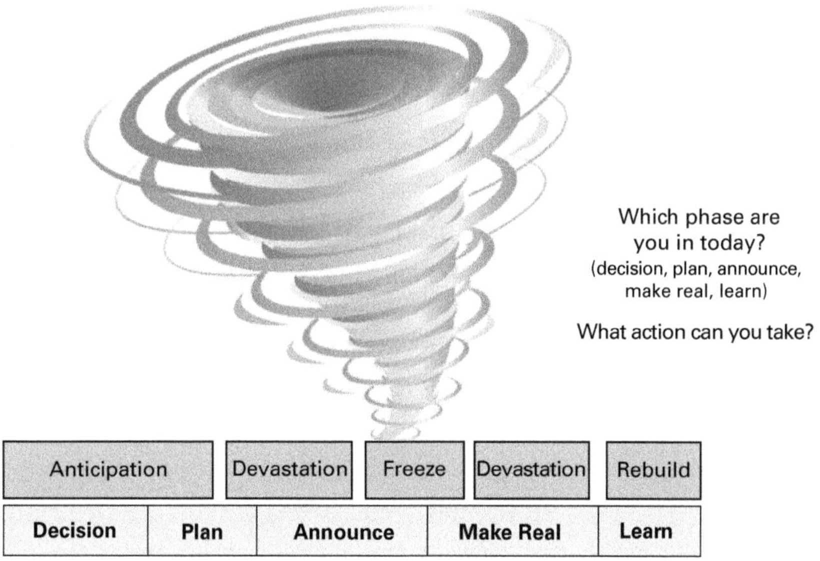

Which phase are
you in today?
(decision, plan, announce,
make real, learn)

What action can you take?

Anticipation	Devastation	Freeze	Devastation	Rebuild
Decision	Plan	Announce	Make Real	Learn

FIGURE 4.3   The Crucial Phases of Change

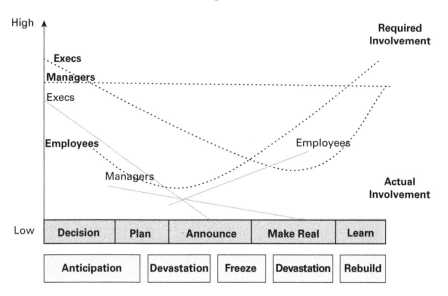

where that may fall short. When you look at the process of a Change Tornado and consider the change cycle you go through, the first step is the decision that change is needed. We are launching a new product, acquiring a new company, changing how we provide support to our customers, etc.

The decision is the first step in the change cycle and that's when anticipation starts. That's when you have already started to trigger excitement, fear, concern, happiness, any one of those emotions, some of them all at the same time for some people. After you make the decision, you then go into the planning phase. After you've gone through the planning phase, you then announce the changes. Then you then have to make it real. After you've made it real, you learn, you look back, and you reflect. Those stages sound so simple to write or read, but in reality they can take months or years of planning, or may be skipped over in minutes. The reason I created this Change Tornado framework was to help leaders see the multiple layers of complexity when communicating significant changes.

Think back to a change that you recently introduced or were part of that someone else introduced. Consider where the CEO or executives got involved: was it before or after the decision was made? What about the managers needing to plan and prepare? What about employees impacted? What the Change Tornado shows is where people typically get involved, and where they should really be involved.

Reflect on a recent significant change for each group—did they get involved at the right time, too early, or too late?

CEO/Executive Sponsor: _____

Executive Leadership Team: _____

Managers: _____

Employees: _____

In any significant change you want to ask these three critical questions:

In deciding:

"Who do we need to involve before we make the decision?**"**

In implementing:

"We have made the decision, who needs
to help with implementation?**"**

In deconstructing success:

"Who should we ask to help evaluate how this went?**"**

Too often I see managers and employees involved too late and executives losing interest too early. There is too much caution around involving managers and employees before a decision has been made when in fact that is exactly who you need to involve, to evaluate if and how to make the decision and the best way to implement it.

The Role of the Chief of Staff

In my corporate career with Microsoft when I was at the recently acquired Rare Games Studio, I was offered a unique role to move to the global headquarters in Redmond, Washington in the US. The role was called a Business Manager, but it fulfilled all of the duties of what evolved to become known as a Chief of Staff position. What seemed like a vague title was in fact one of the most fascinating roles of my career, in the Home and Entertainment Division when the iPod competitor Zune was created, the touch-screen coffee table Microsoft Surface was invented, and Xbox 360 had just launched. My boss, Denise White, also supported what was called the "BillG groups"— effectively all of the groups Bill Gates personally still managed, from Microsoft Research to the Chief Technology Office and the innovation teams. Microsoft, like many other large companies, had its own company vocabulary. When I was first told I would be running the division's "Rhythm of the Business" I did wonder what musical aspect to my job was required! But I soon learned that it was my role to manage the corporate calendar and create all the strategic planning, communication events, and management meetings needed to meet the company and division requirements. It was a rapid way for me to immerse myself into the headquarters of Microsoft, meeting a broad range of executives and functions, and knowing just how the annual calendar and events all came together. The greatest lesson I learned in the two years I held the role was that leaders who surround themselves with people who complement their abilities succeed the most.

Companies like Microsoft and Lenovo use the Chief of Staff term; Amazon uses the term Technical Advisor. Regardless of title, if you don't have a Chief of Staff or Business Manager on your executive team, consider who will perform the following activities as they will accelerate the impact of your communications:

- coordinating the company calendar;
- being the glue between functions and individuals;
- guiding the strategy and future planning;
- keeping track of cross-functional projects;

– holding the bar for performance high;

– driving accountability for delivery of commitments;

– ensuring communication mechanisms are in place.

This role is one of the most pivotal on an executive team; not only does it relieve the CEO of these activities, it provides a fascinating growth accelerator role for a high-performing leader looking to expand their career.

Now we have explored the power of internal communications. Next, we will understand how you can put your customer at the heart of your company.

05

Customers at the Heart of Your Company

Customers know when you are being fake and when you are speaking from your heart. Cookie-cutter communications no longer work. With endless data points and insights about your customers, CEOs have to create nuanced communication that is honest, authentic, and meaningful. It starts with finding your *raison d'être*, the ultimate reason for your own existence and that of your company. This drives your strategy, behavior, and communication. This chapter shares innovative examples of CEOs making unique connections with their customers, defining customer-centric strategies, communicating in unusual ways, and embracing technology and old-fashioned methods alike to build an endless loyalty loop with customers.

CHAPTER TOPICS

- Creating Unexpected Experiences
- Immersing Yourself in Your Customer's Life
- Understanding Your Company and Personal Purpose
- The Power of the Written Word
- Top Ten Customer Crisis Questions to Ask

Creating Unexpected Experiences

At the precise moment airlines want you to pay attention, 95 percent of customers look away. Safety demonstrations are hardly the most exciting or eye-catching, and if you look around the cabin when the emergency instructions are being explained, almost everyone is looking elsewhere. But Air New Zealand is different. I will never forget my first flight with them from Los Angeles to England: every single passenger was watching the screen. Every flight I have taken with them since has made me appreciate their innovative approaches that prove how they put their customers at the heart of their company.

1. Catch your customer's attention

Air New Zealand does this by using championship surfers to give safety instructions from a beautiful beach while surfing. Their safety demonstration looked like the start of a movie. This made sure that every passenger's attention was captured. A company's communication to customers and employees can be tedious and predictable, so it's important to ask:

"How can we create the unexpected?"

2. Make the usually bland exciting

Why don't other airlines decorate the drab and dreary airplane bathrooms? Air New Zealand's bathrooms have chandeliers, bookcases, and amusing window displays at the marginal cost of a few decal stickers. It is brilliantly creative. Walk (or fly!) a mile in your customers' shoes, follow their customer journey through the minutia of each interaction with everyone in your company, and then ask yourself:

"How can this step be more entertaining and exciting?"

3. Make sure your customers are sitting comfortably

Airline seats are notoriously uncomfortable, as the economies of flying involve having as many people as possible in the smallest space possible. Even so, minor changes can make a significant difference. Someone figured out that one of the most uncomfortable parts of flying if you aren't particularly tall is the pressure of the chair on your legs. Air New Zealand provides its premium economy passengers with small beanbags to rest their feet on. Likely more economical than integrated full footrests, these provide comfort at a reasonable cost. As you reflect on this with your team, ask:

"How can we make our customers more comfortable?"

4. Experiment with new designs

Not every new design concept will work the first time. There are touted new airplane designs, such as hexagon-style seating designed to increase the number of passengers per square inch in each plane and other configurations to achieve the same. But Air New Zealand bucked the trend and chose the opposite direction, with their seats in premium economy that point away from each other for additional privacy and space. When you compare yourself to your competition, ask your team:

"How can we throw out the conventional and experiment?"

5. Have real conversations

Customer surveys with tick sheets and click boxes are not compelling. Customers rarely complete them, and when they are completed, what does a rating of 3.75 out of 5 mean in terms of specific praise or opportunities for improvement? At the end of my Air New Zealand flight, an attendant came and sat by me with a blank notebook and pen. She smiled and explained she wanted my feedback, asking about my flight and the service provided by Vera, my flight attendant. We had a real conversation, just like I was talking to a friend. I told specific real stories that were detailed, and there was not a number or score in sight! She told me that they shared the specific feedback with their attendants as soon as they disembarked because it motivated the team to hear immediate stories about their impact. When you reflect on what you know about your customers, ask:

> **"**How can we ask real questions
> and get specific answers back that we can act on?**"**

6. Match need and investment

This is my favorite customer differentiator, probably because I do like to take risks and occasionally gamble and this time it paid off for me! On the flight back to Los Angeles I was given the opportunity to bid for an upgrade to business class for myself and my then seven-year-old daughter. I bid a few hundred dollars and was told my bid was unlikely to result in an upgrade. To my delight, a few days before my return journey I was told my bid had been accepted. I loved this eBay approach to bidding what you are prepared to invest in an enhanced experience. Air New Zealand gets to maximize revenue opportunities, and passengers get to decide how they want to enhance their journey. What ideas does this create for you? Consider this question with your team:

> **"**How can we provide innovative
> ways for our customers to invest more?**"**

I now plan my European travel around the flight schedule with Air New Zealand. I have also told this story and shared these lessons with thousands of people at conferences; I am clearly a loyal fan and amplifier of a company that knows how to put their customer at the heart of their company. Figure 5.1 is an Unexpected Experiences tool you can use with your teams to ask them to imagine the possibilities

FIGURE 5.1 Unexpected Experiences Tool

CATCH ATTENTION
BLAND → EXCITING
SITTING COMFORTABLY
NEW DESIGNS
REAL CONVERSATIONS
NEED VS. INVESTMENT

of an enhanced customer experience in your company. As you reflect on what you can do to create unexpected experiences for your own customers, let's explore some additional examples of CEOs putting their customer right at the heart of their company by immersing themselves in their customer's whole life.

Immersing Yourself in Your Customer's Life

Steven Webster is CEO of asensei, a technology company creating sportswear that tracks your progress and gives you real-time coaching feedback. Earlier in his entrepreneurial life he sold his company to Adobe and built out Adobe's worldwide consulting division. Here's what Steven shared about how he encouraged his whole organization to embed themselves alongside their customers to create the greatest performance possible:

> The soul of the organization we created was using the idea of "design-led innovation," which we believed sat in the intersection of business, technology, and design. We started every engagement with a project that was more about ethnography and anthropology than it was about technology. We'd spend the first two or three weeks of a project living a day in the life of our target user and building as much empathy and understanding for that user as possible.

We were asked by NATO to help them with the workflow for mission planning. It was a very document-oriented process, lots of paper and printouts, something that a company that builds workflows around PDFs and electronic documents should be able to come in and solve. I had a team of my designers set out for an airforce base in Geilenkirchen, a small German town on the border of The Netherlands. There was data entry, an excessive amount of data entry, pieces of paper coming out of one part of the process and being rekeyed into another part of the process. I had user-experience designers fly on the AWACS aircraft, so they could see how this data entry would be carried on a huge disk and loaded into the plane to configure the plane for a reconnaissance or security operation. Then there was the key moment when we were invited to a mission planning and found members of the military with scissors, sellotape, and maps. They were cutting bits of maps apart and gluing them together into fictional landscapes, creating new lands, and loading them into the system. Drawing no-fly zones with pen and paper, drawing targets, drawing whatever, and this was the source of all of this data that was being keyed and rekeyed and reentered.

It was the soul of the experience.

We created a mission-planning system that was no longer about efficiently moving PDFs and electronic records through an organization but was anchored in a highly visual ability to draw and create and annotate maps while pulling data behind the scenes from over eighty different systems. The fleeting observation of people preparing missions by stitching rolled-up maps on top of a filing cabinet revealed the solution to us.

In another project, I was asked to fix Adobe's own customer support organization. Our CSAT (customer satisfaction) scores were pointing in the wrong direction around the launch of Adobe's Creative Cloud product, and the presumption was that because CSAT was related to our call center performance, we should shift customers to self-service applications. But to really understand the problem, we sent our designers to work in the call centers—in Manilla, and in Amsterdam. We put them through training as call center agents for a week, and then we had them sit on the phone and answer and resolve calls. It was there that we uncovered all manner of insights (some that I can tell here, and others I cannot!) into the inefficiencies and workarounds our agents had invented that were leading to poor customer satisfaction in the call center.

We built a special room in San Jose where we could invite executives to sit on a chat queue and answer support enquiries themselves for their own products. Decisions that may have seemed trivial in a leadership meeting—what's the policy and process for an educational discount?—compared to the more exciting new product features for photo manipulation suddenly would get escalated. Why are we asking students to fax their student card to a call center and wait until it's manually reconciled before we approve their educational discount? Their term project is due tomorrow!

By allowing everyone in the organization—from the CEO to the VPs of product management and the engineers building the product—to experience a day in the life of the customer or user, we were able to build deep empathy that informed technology decisions and business processes alike (like educational discount policies).

It's something I've carried through with me to asensei. When we decided that high school rowers were a target customer for us, we ran a workshop at Serra High School in the Bay Area to really understand the challenges a high school rower faces that asensei could fix. We don't have a support team at asensei, or rather it's two of the company founders, myself and my chief product officer. If you email support@asensei.com because your password won't reset or you can't connect asensei to your rowing machine or you are using our product because you're recovering from a knee injury and can't run anymore, then it's one of the founders that's answering your email. That close contact and empathy with the customer is what informs our business priorities and our technology roadmap.

What I love most about the stories Steven tells is that whether you are dealing with mission-critical NATO planning, a customer service helpdesk for a technology company, or an interactive rowing machine, the principles are the same: you must consider the customer in your strategy, your communication, and your behavior. If any one of those areas is missing, you will not be as profitable. This is shown in the Ultimate Customer Profit Lens in Figure 5.2.

FIGURE 5.2   Ultimate Customer Profit Lens

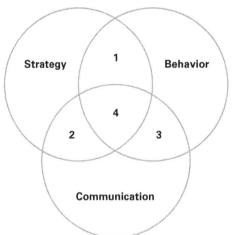

1. Hidden brilliance
2. False promises
3. Disjointed random acts
4. Profit and performance accelerated

All three factors—hidden brilliance, false promises, and disjointed random acts—have to be intentionally addressed to maximize your profit and performance. This is why many efforts to improve communication fail, because often it isn't the communication that is the issue, it is the strategy or behavior of team members that causes efforts to slow down. Consider where your company has strength, and where you have opportunities to improve.

Hidden Brilliance

If you have a strong strategy immersed in your customer coupled with the right behaviors of your team, yet lack communication, then that is where you are missing out on many more customers and the resulting profit. It is like you are a best-kept secret. You need to identify how to communicate in new ways more consistently to let your brilliance show. It is time to ask:

"How does our customer want to hear from us and how often?**"**

False Promises

If you have a robust strategy and brilliant communication but the behaviors of your team don't live up to the expectations you set, then you will create disappointed customers. Your false promises will cause your customers to leave you and not return, so it is important to evaluate what behaviors need to change to allow reality to meet your promises. Ask the managers in your company this question:

> **"**What behaviors are important to our customers and how do we improve?**"**

Disjointed Random Acts

If you have exemplary behavior toward your customer and your communication is perfected but your strategy is lacking, then you will appear confusing to your customer. While they may be delighted with each interaction, it won't necessarily lead to a return visit or additional spend, because you aren't being intentional. It all might feel a little random. It's time for you to consider this:

> **"**What is our intention with our customers and how will we achieve that?**"**

The ultimate prize is where you have a strong intentional strategy, clear behaviors defined and demonstrated, and unique communication that captures your customers' attention and loyalty. Before diving into more examples, let's look at the value of being grounded in your company purpose.

Understanding Your Company and Personal Purpose

In Chapter 4 we explored how to define and unlock your personal purpose, which is an important first step before creating your company purpose. Many of you reading this may be in a role where your company purpose is already defined for you, or you may be part of an executive team that is on the journey of defining who you are and what your *raison d'être* really is.

The Purpose Pyramid in Chapter 4 can be used for defining your company purpose too. If you jumped straight to this chapter, it will be helpful for you to take a look at the Personal Purpose Pyramid first, and then return to review this Company Purpose Pyramid as shown in Figure 5.3.

The seven layers of the Company Purpose Pyramid allow you to extract and build your company purpose and story. When I work with executive teams, individual members of the team create their own Purpose Pyramid before working on the company one as it allows us to build the unique stories of the executives into the overall purpose of the company.

FIGURE 5.3   Your Company Purpose Pyramid

Let's start with the first layer: defining history. Depending on how recently everyone joined the executive team, consider how well everyone understands the company's history. Knowing how your company was founded, any changes of ownership, IPO, acquisition, expansion, contraction, difficulties, and changes in leadership helps you understand the past. When I start working with a new client, I love to ask who has been at the company the longest as I find incredible value in hearing their perspectives on change of leadership, ownership, past successes, and previous mistakes. A creative way to unlock this is by asking:

"If we were a museum exhibit, what would be on display?"

Next, in the second step you need to collectively define your values, or review your existing company values if they are already defined. You can discover them by asking this question:

"What do we truly care about and expect of others?"

The third step is stating your *raison d'être*, or your reason for being. This is where you can describe your why or your purpose through the following question:

"Why are we here, why do we matter?"

In the fourth step you will commit to what your customers can expect from you—what you will consistently deliver. You can do that by finishing this sentence:

"Every customer can always..."

A further commitment comes in the fifth layer, when you consider your employees. What do you want every one of your team members to be able to rely on as they work at your company? Starting with these words can help you articulate this:

"Our commitment to our employees is...**"**

Next, you want to declare how your customers will engage with you, and how you will listen to them, hear them, and act on their feedback. It starts by saying:

"We are listening, here is how...**"**

These layers create the foundation that allows you to create your company soundbites—the phrases you will use in your marketing, media, and internal communications. Many companies start at this seventh step, which is where the empty rhetoric and glib phrases come in.

Never was this more pronounced than during the social justice movement in 2020 following the murder of George Floyd by Derek Chauvin. Companies reacted to Black Lives Matter protests with glib responses on social media that were not backed up by their actions or investments. But employees and customers expect better than that: they want companies to show more of who they are by declaring their purpose and what is important to them as a company. The new expectations mean that CEOs and companies have to decide what foundation they build their purpose on and when to take a stand versus staying silent. Customers and employees are demanding it.

This Company Purpose Pyramid allows you to align your executive team, board, and employees around who you are and how you put customers at the heart of your business. This will allow you to stand out in all the right ways.

The Power of the Written Word

My English teacher Mr. Potts would now be very proud of me; at this point I know that I wasn't the easiest student when he taught me in my teenage years. Now that I know I have an ADHD brain, I can see that that likely contributed to the difficulty I had putting my ideas on paper right at the moment that he wanted me to. In my retail career, writing didn't matter to store profitability, nor did it matter in car manufacturing, IT consulting, telecommunications, or healthcare. Once I joined Microsoft, I had to create a visual story through PowerPoint and spreadsheets—their communication vehicles of choice. But when I arrived at Amazon on their Fashion Leadership team, I encountered the writing challenge that made me feel like I was back in my English class as a teenager!

I credit Amazon with teaching me to write concisely and with impact. The toughest part of my transition from my Microsoft corporate life to Amazon was learning to write convincingly and thoroughly in a narrative that put the customer and long-term shareholder value first. I'm grateful now for that lesson, and it is one of the recommendations I give my clients: use the power of the written word because fancy diagrams don't always work. When you are forced to write, in detail, with facts, it causes you to pause. It is easy to hand-wave through a slick presentation with promises and wild claims.

At Amazon a document is prepared for every decision, investment, strategy review, or new idea, and it is put together with the customer in mind. These documents are prepared in advance of a meeting. When you arrive at the meeting, the six-pager is distributed for everyone to read, in silence. Everyone takes notes on the document, and the meeting owner will then ask everyone to go page by page through it to answer questions or hear comments. I loved this approach because it gives everyone an equal voice and accounts for different styles of absorbing and processing information. It also stops attendees from echoing the opinion of whoever is the most senior or talks the loudest, which can happen when a leader dominates a decision or discussion. Amazon uses this approach to ensure that the customer is considered for every investment. I created the Brilliant Business Case and Rapid Scoping Plan as a tool to help companies define their initiatives through the eyes of the customer and create a shared understanding of the impact of new initiatives.

BRILLIANT BUSINESS CASE AND RAPID SCOPING PLAN

This is the tool I use to help companies create their own new initiatives, and we can walk through it each step of the way so that after reading this part of the chapter you will have a solid business case for any new idea you are considering.

1. Summary—the quick overview that explains the overall pitch

Purpose: *One-line purpose of the new initiative/product/service.*

Detailed Description: *Include any specific details of the product/service.*

Timing: *High-level timing (e.g., H2 FY22).*

Executive Sponsor: *Which leadership team member is sponsoring this initiative?*

2. Starting at the end—fast-forward to launch and describe what you see

Press Release: *Write the press release, with the headline, detailed article, and publication it would be featured in.*

Customer Reactions: *What will our customers say in reaction to this?*

Associate Reactions: *What will our associates say and feel?*

Board Update: *What will be the report to the board if this is a success?*

3. Today and the future—the six steps of scoping—the detailed work to scope the initiative

	Today	Future
1 Customers	Is this for our existing customers or attracting a new different customer? What is in place today for customers? What do they experience? What is their current feedback? What customer metrics support this initiative?	Who is the new customer? What would be the customer experience / opportunity? What would change in how our customer experiences us? What customer metrics would demonstrate success?

	Today	Future
2 Competition	What is our competition already doing in this space today? What competitive data do we have or do we need to gather? Are we currently behind, on par, ahead, or best in class in this area?	What do we know or suspect our competition will launch in the future? What is our goal, do we want to be behind, on par, ahead, or best in class in this area?
3 Speed	Until now, how rapidly have we addressed this in the past?	What is the proposed speed of implementation? What is the cost of doing nothing?
4 Costs	What are the current costs: budgeted, overspend, etc.	What are the total cost implications of this initiative?
5 Revenue	What is the current revenue associated with this initiative today?	What is the anticipated net revenue increase as a result of this initiative?
6 Profit	What is the current profit associated with this initiative today? What financial metrics track current status?	What is the future predicted profit associated with this initiative over what time period? What financial metrics will track future success?

4. Capability and capacity assessment

- What capabilities do we need to finalize the business case, develop the implementation plan, and launch the product?
- Do you have those resources today, and when are they free to start work on this product?
- What cross-functional support is needed?
- Where do you have gaps?

5. Implementation planning

- What key dates/milestones are important?
- What internal or external factors might disrupt the course of this work (e.g., legislative, reliance on strategic partnerships, lack of technology resources)?
  - o Internal –
  - o External –

- What are your top ideas for mitigating these?

- Who are the key stakeholders who need to be involved?

6. Best reasons not to do this

Of course, this is your initiative, and you believe in it and want to make it happen. If you were looking at this objectively and critically, what would be the best reasons not to do this, or not to do this in the time horizon you propose?

Once you have completed your Brilliant Business Case and Rapid Scoping Plan, you should have enough input to pitch your idea to your board, CEO, or boss. I'd love to hear your feedback after using this tool yourself. What insights did it give you? If you skipped ahead to this section wondering whether it is worth working through this, I want to share some insights a financial services company gave me after we completed this exercise as part of their three-year strategic planning:

- "We grew up in an undisciplined environment, and business cases are helping us become more disciplined. I want to learn how to do this well."

- "James was always more disciplined than us. This is helping us be more like James."

- "Initially I struggled, but I am seeing a lot of value from walking through one of them with one project and then doing them for my own products."

- "Business cases helped me realize we can't do the expansion work without resolving the current issue. This process has helped the team become more engaged."

- "I usually think big picture, and Sarah is in the weeds. This forced me to get in the weeds and dig in. I know I'm the guy who keeps saying, let's try this, which can be maddening; I love how this forces me to talk about how it affects customers."

- "This forces me to not only think six chess moves ahead but to put in the guard rails and stop thinking fluffy, but make it real."

- "It forces 360 thinking, so you are not just thinking about your area but every area you might touch."
- "The focus on the board update and the press release keeps you centered, and forces shared understanding and clarity."
- "Sharing across the different teams yesterday showed how much we need to discuss cross-function to get a shared understanding of what we are trying to achieve."
- "We need to devote more time to working across teams. This is helping to get everyone on the same page."

WORDS THAT WORK DECONSTRUCTION

Note what I am doing here: I am using tactics to teach you how you can work with your customers. I am sharing my customer feedback on one of my products to help other customers (you the reader) see the value of what I bring. How are you using your own customers to encourage other customers and help them use your products and services more?

Top Ten Customer Crisis Questions to Ask

Putting your customers at the heart of your company isn't always easy. A crisis is the very time you want to reset your customer relationship and ask yourself what you can be doing to support your customers during unexpected times. Here is a sample of questions I shared with executives I worked with when the pandemic hit in 2020. Each of these questions was designed to be considered with the customer in mind:

1 How are we protecting our employees' lives or making them easier?
2 Which policies can we temporarily change to help our employees or customers?
3 How can we make it easier for customers to buy from us?
4 What channels could make our customers' lives easier? (For instance, preparing restaurants for drive-through and collection only.[1])

5 What regions do we need to address differently?

6 What innovative ideas do we have that we can rapidly accelerate to help us right now?

7 Do we have the right two-way communication mechanisms in place with our employees and customers?

8 How can we keep our customers loyal to us? (For instance, protecting customer loyalty status during the period of reduced travel.[2])

9 How can we provide an optimistic, realistic, and worst-case scenario plan for how this might affect our business so we can keep our board and investors apprised of the possibilities and realities in the short and long term?

10 What customer-supporting best practices can we learn from?

Now that we have explored how to put your customer at the heart of your company, we have to imagine the impossible by shattering all preconceived ideas and constraints and shooting for the moonshot!

Endnotes

1 Lucas, A (2020) Starbucks CEO says customers may only be able to order via drive-thru or mobile due to coronavirus, *CNBC*, https://www.cnbc.com/2020/03/12/starbucks-may-require-orders-via-drive-thru-mobile-due-to-coronavirus.html (archived at https://perma.cc/HWQ3-4RBR)

2 Nassetta, C (2020) Hilton's response to novel coronavirus, *LinkedIn*, https://www.linkedin.com/pulse/hiltons-response-novel-coronavirus-covid-19-chris-nassetta/?trackingId=0RRhWQhrJxCGX6RN2yTOKQ%3D%3D (archived at https://perma.cc/7MNH-6D8X)

06

It's a Lovely Day for a Moonshot

An offsite event does not create innovation, and hiring a consulting firm does not guarantee that you will unlock big, bold ideas. This chapter explains just how to create moonshot ideas in your company. If you're not familiar with what a moonshot is, quite simply in business it means to have a long-term goal for your company, and this can sometimes be a quite audacious goal. The term *moonshot* came to be when President Kennedy called for human exploration of the moon; it means a humongous problem that requires significant investment of time and resources with innovative thinking. Like that first moonshot, the very idea of a moonshot requires you to suspend belief, to imagine the possibilities, to challenge assumptions, to check your ego at the door, to open your mind, and to involve key decision-makers. From Xbox's fastest-selling device of all time, to babies in space, to the way companies rapidly reinvented themselves throughout the Covid-19 pandemic, this chapter's examples will illuminate the possibilities for you. They provide you with the language, retorts, and comebacks needed to overcome any cynic in your company whose common answer is, "we have tried that, and it didn't work."

CHAPTER TOPICS

- Myths About Moonshots Debunked
- Questions That Generate Big, Bold Ideas
- Why Moonshots Love a Crisis

- Overcoming Resistance When Shooting for the Moon
- Ten Powerful Positive Retorts
- Get Your Head in the Moonshot Game
- Competitions Encourage Moonshots
- Your Personal Moonshot

If there was one lesson from this chapter to learn, this would be it:

> **"** No, I won't help you with an
> offsite event, because that's not what you need! **"**

Myths About Moonshots Debunked

Perhaps you have jumped to this chapter because you have a two-day retreat scheduled with your executive team, or your top fifty executives and you are looking for some tips for creating moonshot ideas. Perhaps your CEO has asked for big, bold ideas for achieving your five-year strategy. Perhaps you've invested heavily in outside experts to create an innovation program that is floundering, and you need some direction. I'm here for it all.

An example of moonshots in action can be seen in the halls of the Consumer Electronics Show that takes place every January in Las Vegas. This is the innovation trade show that showcases products and technology with varying degrees of possibility and probability of changing our lives. BrainCo Dexus previewed a prosthetic hand that you control with electrical signals from your brain; groundbreaking for amputees if the prototype becomes a reality. I love to track down such ambitious projects to see just where they are now, and indeed they are progressing well. The product was spun off into its own company, Brain Robotics, and it's awaiting approval from the Food and Drug Administration in the US and then onto mass production.

Not all moonshots follow such a positive path. In 2018, at one of my favorite innovation events, Harvest Summit, a far more radical and thought-provoking moonshot was revealed: Space Origin, a Dutch start-up, announced plans for the first baby to be born in space by 2024. It certainly was a conversation starter and caused many to pause and consider the possibilities and implications. By 2019 the company had wound up its operations, citing, according to a statement posted by CEO Kees Mulder on the company's website, there were "serious ethical, safety, and medical concerns" that caused him to suspend the two missions planning to safely conceive and deliver babies in space.

There are three myths about moonshots that we need to debunk before continuing.

First, the idea that **every company needs** a moonshot is wrong. While Silicon Valley and corporations around the world may have adopted the phrase as their own, having a moonshot in your strategy is not a prerequisite for success. Quite the opposite. Instead say:

> **"**We will focus on our known strategies and implement them flawlessly.**"**

The second myth is the idea that **we have to hire consultants.** I realize the phrase "no one ever got fired for hiring McKinsey" is common for a reason, but you can create your own moonshot program without a seven-figure investment in outside help. Instead say:

> **"**Who do we have internally, and do we even need outside help?**"**

Finally, the myth that we **have a dedicated leader for this** is a guaranteed way to make it fail. Moonshot ideas will never succeed if your CEO or CFO abdicate responsibility to another leader from the start. Instead say:

> **"**As an executive team here's how we will each support this...**"**

Questions That Generate Big, Bold Ideas

With your Company Purpose Pyramid from Chapter 5 as a foundation, use the following questions to provoke and inspire big, bold ideas:

"What has no one else tried?**"**

"What could be possible and probable?**"**

"What are we uniquely positioned to create?**"**

"Which other countries are ahead of the curve on this?**"**

"If we weren't concerned about failing, what would we do?**"**

"What is changing in our customers' lives that we can support?**"**

"What technology exists in other industries that we could use?**"**

"If we had an unexpected $1,000,000
to invest, where would we spend it?**"**

Why Moonshots Love a Crisis

Big, blue-sky thinking is delightful on a relaxed sunny day when business is stable, growing, and everyone has time to contemplate and plan. But oddly enough, a pending or real crisis creates a different dynamic where moonshots seem to prosper.

Unfortunately, at Xbox, it took a billion-dollar write-off for "create a broad appeal Xbox" to become an internal rally cry. During my corporate career with Xbox, I was fortunate to be part of the small team that created an innovation experience to explore how we could catch up to Nintendo and PlayStation in the battle for the gaming customer and the future of living room entertainment.

The result was the Kinect camera, which launched in 2010 and sold 10 million devices in three months, making it the fastest-selling consumer electronics device of all time, earning a place in the *Guinness World Records book*. While the Kinect may no longer be in production in its original form, its technology is now used in many Microsoft products. Its greatest impact has been beyond entertainment, in the medical field, enabling doctors to use simple hand gestures to change, move, or zoom in on CT scans, MRIs, and other medical images to make surgery faster and more accurate.

The Covid-19 pandemic launched many moonshots. Successful companies took the crisis as an opportunity to give back and support their customers and communities. Some of my favorite success stories born from this crisis have been:

- James Dyson, who invented the Dyson revolutionary vacuum cleaner, received a call from British Prime Minister Boris Johnson who said, "You have manufacturing plants. You are an inventor. How can you help us get ventilators?" Fourteen days later, Dyson had figured out a way; he created a prototype in that small window of time, and they accelerated all of the usual endorsements and checks and had a plan to make 15,000 ventilators. It is interesting to note that the UK government decided the ventilators were no longer required, but what a testament to how quickly a company can adapt and create a moonshot moment in a dire time of need.

- Canada Goose adapted their factories to produce hospital scrubs and gowns as they were in short supply.

- Belkin International adapted their factories from making computer and phone accessories to making emergency ventilators in partnership with the University of Illinois.

- NASA's Jet Propulsion Laboratory developed a new ventilator in thirty-seven days.

- Apple designed and manufactured face shields for health workers.

- Four Seasons led the way in New York when they stated that healthcare workers should not be going home to their families, potentially spreading the virus. They opened up their hotels. This led to a further five hotels following suit in twenty-four hours, and they became the beacon of support for healthcare workers in the city.

My final example is a personal one, and a story of multiple connections. Early in the pandemic, I was picking up lunch for my family at a local café, and I overheard the customer in front of me explain that she was working in a local hospital. I asked her whether they were struggling with supplies as had been reported. She confirmed it and explained that they were cutting wipes in half and were low on other supplies. She told me her husband worked there too, so both were exposed. At that point my propensity to help kicked in, which resulted in this chain of events:

- It occurred to me that one of my clients, Belkin, is owned by Foxconn. Foxconn, a Chinese manufacturer, had pivoted their factory a couple of months earlier from making gadgets and widgets and pieces of manufacturing parts to making masks.
- I called their CIO, explained the situation, and asked how we could make the right connections; he offered to connect the Foxconn team.
- Next, I happened to see on LinkedIn that an executive I'd met at a Los Angeles Chamber of Commerce event seven years earlier was sharing that he had business contacts who had a surplus of masks.
- The final connection was asking a local council member who I knew was connected to the CEO of the hospital for the best way to contact her.
- With her contact details and several potential sources of personal protection equipment, I was able to share resources and contacts with the CEO of the hospital.

"What moonshot stories can
you tell where you connected the dots?**"**

I share this multistep story because the art of connecting dots can overcome what feels like the gargantuan task of a moonshot. The more relevant connections you have, the more likely you are to have people you can help or connect others to. This further emphasizes the value of keeping your network hydrated, as discussed in Chapter 3. While this case was to solve a catastrophic problem, the deeper and broader your connections, the more valuable you will be as an executive—and the greater the opportunity for strategic partnerships allowing you to tackle moonshots together. Regularly ask your team this:

"Who do you know in these companies or industries that we can meet?"

The unique opportunity a crisis gives you is a chance to reset. Stability and repetition are the greatest barriers to achieving moonshots. In a crisis you can more easily ask a question like this:

"If you were to reinvent your company today, what would you change?"

Imagine you had a blank sheet of paper and considered your customer, their current and future needs, and your company's unique expertise, technology, and assets. Consider what your company blueprint would look like and how you would go to market. A crisis creates a shift in mindset, generating a whatever-it-takes mentality that allows a freedom to imagine the possibilities.

If you have changed companies or moved jobs since the Covid-19 crisis began, ask those around you to tell their stories of how your current company responded, adapted, and innovated during the pandemic.

"What changed at our company during the Covid-19 pandemic?"

That will allow you to understand the company history and the defining experiences of those around you, which helps you strengthen your understanding of the company purpose and that of those around you. This deeper understanding will help you as you prepare for the inevitable when you are driving big, bold ideas—those who resist you—which we will explore next.

Overcoming Resistance When Shooting for the Moon

Contrarians are wonderful because they may point out what you cannot see, so channel any exhaustion you may feel as they relentlessly poke holes in your ideas and suggestions. I was working with a CEO of a technology company as he was preparing to give a talk at the company strategy retreat with the top 100 executives. His biggest concern was the questions he would get from the audience and how best to respond, as he was proposing some audacious new initiatives and asking for and expecting feedback. I prepared this cheat sheet of Ten Powerful Positive Retorts for the feedback he might receive.

Ten Powerful Positive Retorts

Feedback	Positive Retort
"We've tried that before."	"I'd love to understand more…"
"It is just too complex to solve."	"Let's explore what parts are complex…"
"The last three times that failed."	"I'm curious what was different…"
"Our competition is doing it faster/better."	"What do they do that we don't?"
"Your assumptions are wrong."	"Let's meet separately so I can hear more…"
"Why are you convinced you can make this work?"	"I'm confident that we can, are you?"
"We are wasting our time exploring this."	"What could we do instead?"
"No one believes this will work."	"For all the same reasons, or different ones?"
"The risks are too high."	"If we overcome them, what is the upside?"
"This isn't the right way."	"Tell me more."

With three tweens/teenagers in our house, I have learned the power of the retort, but at work it needs to have a positive angle. I'd love to hear other contrarian feedback you receive as you explore your moonshots. Text me yours and let me know you are reading Chapter 6 in the book, and I will give you a personalized positive retort. It will help you prepare for considering big, bold ideas. To do that you need to get your head in the right place.

Get Your Head in the Moonshot Game

To lead your company or team through moonshots and bold, audacious goals you need to be in the right headspace. Get out of your usual circles and typical venues. Find new circles to join, events that may be tangential to your industry or functional expertise. I always encourage the CMOs I work with to attend technology events, and vice versa for the technology executives. Consider your weekly reading homework, what publications you are immersing yourself in, what appears in your mailbox, both digitally and physically, and which podcasts, TV shows, and interactive conversations you are participating in. Every week experiment with a new topic to learn about the world; keep your curiosity high when you are out of your knowledge and expertise depth.

Jolt thinking, listen to Louie Schwartzberg's *7 Minutes of Gratitude Revealed*, listen to music, swap your usual chair, stand rather than sit, walk and talk—do anything to shift the predictable to the possible. At the inaugural innovation event Harvest Summit, I did something I had never done before and likely will never do again: I sang at the start of my talk! Luckily, there were three of us singing together, but it was part of creating an unexpected moment. Myself and two other innovation experts appeared from three different corners of the room, all singing "It's a marvelous day for a moonshot" to the backing music of Van Morrison's "Moondance." It certainly was unexpected; the audience members were twisting and turning in their chairs trying to figure out what was happening for those thirty seconds of spontaneous singing. Even though TV producer Mark

Burnett was also speaking at that innovation event and there is no danger of any of us giving up our day jobs for a singing career, the unusual interlude captured attention. How could you create an unexpected moment before your next moonshot conversation?

Competitions Encourage Moonshots

A $1 million prize for a competition may seem excessive to some, but consider the value that you create for a company and it becomes an equitable share of the impact you can create. Online real-estate company Zillow launched a $1 million prize in 2017 for anyone who could figure out how to improve the accuracy of one of its algorithms that predicts home values. Groups of data scientists around the world competed for the prize, broadening the brain power of new machine-learning techniques that a small internal team alone could never have mastered. Two years later, Zillow followed through on their promise and awarded the seven-figure prize to the winning team, who had beaten Zillow's own internal team by 13 percent.[1]

Daymond John launched Black Entrepreneurs Day in October 2020—right in the heart of the Covid-19 pandemic when many were still unable to leave their homes apart from for essential trips. This five-hour online event was the most impressive virtual event I have ever attended. He had musicians perform live mini-concerts. Minority entrepreneurs were featured throughout the event. There was a grant competition where the winners in various categories were announced throughout the event. I hosted a watch party for one of my clients, and as a result, two business deals were made from virtual introductions that never would have happened otherwise.

Womenswear retailer francesca's launched a Fran Finds competition to find new entrepreneurs to feature in their boutiques and online store. This was a strategy to demonstrate their *Free to Be You* philosophy, to achieve their goal of finding and celebrating originality with new vendors. This provides support for up-and-coming creators to grow their business within francesca's ecosystem. After the initial application phase, a shortlist of applicants were to be invited to the francesca's headquarters to participate in a *Shark Tank*-style pitch competition to win one of three places. EVP of Merchandising Victoria Taylor explained to me that they would be more like a Bunny Hutch than a Shark Tank as the judges would be kinder and more supportive than the Sharks on the ABC hit show! Victoria shared more about the why behind the initiative:

> This helps us add diversity, women-owned brands, supporting people that started businesses up during the pandemic. We're now in the process of contacting each of these twenty people, inviting them to Bunny Hutch Day, and they'll be coming for two days to present a panel. From there, we will pick three winners who we will then start working with. Not only will we be buying their product, we will also be providing them with mentorship—professional coaching, how to set up their marketing, how to source better, how to run their business.

As one of the judges for the Fran Finds competition it was remarkable how a factor in the successful pitches was using Words That Worked. At the time of writing I can't yet announce the winner, but the way in which the entrepreneurs put the customer at the heart of their business as discussed in Chapter 5, and how they shared their Purpose Pyramid, made their products rise to the top and their stories stand out. If you are curious to learn more, go to www.wrightwordsthatwork.com and I will post the winners and their stories for you to hear.

Consider how you can think about your business in a radically different way. The CEO of Xbox once said to me when I was part of the leadership team, "Val, you come up with lots of big, crazy ideas and I might not always like all of them, but don't stop them coming. There is usually a pretty good ratio of ideas to acceptance."

Make sure you have idea generators on your team and that you are tapping into them. Make sure that in your team meetings, you are creating open space to help your teams think: What if? What could we do? What talent do we have? What machinery do we have? What supply chain or channels or expertise do we have? How can we pivot that? Because then you can figure out how you can best put your company talent to use.

Your Personal Moonshot

During one of those company moonshot moments at Xbox, as I hit my twenty-fifth anniversary in corporate life, I had a surprising moonshot idea of my own. I had founded my first company at age fifteen as part of an HSBC-sponsored competition with the Young Enterprise Scheme in England. I then immersed myself in corporate life. It occurred to me that my own moonshot would be to run my own business and write a book. All of the finalists at the Fran Finds competition that I judged explained their self-doubt, hesitancy, and caution, yet they proceeded anyway and they all have products, revenue, a purpose, and a dream. So, how are you considering your own moonshot possibilities?

Finding the right words that give you the desired results in every situation does not always come naturally or easily for many; it can drain the energy out of you and cause your emotions to unexpectedly flare. Let's explore next just how you can learn to love your emotions, even the ones you think you should not.

Endnote

1 Gagliordi, N (2019) Zillow awards $1 million to data scientists for improving its Zestimate algorithm, *ZDNET*, https://www.zdnet.com/article/zillow-awards-1-million-to-data-scientists-for-improving-its-zestimate-algorithm/ (archived at https://perma.cc/C5YD-GGA3)

07

How to Love Your Anger
and Other Emotions

If you have never met an angry CEO or executive, then you haven't met many of them. Knowing how to handle your own anger or that of those you work with, especially if it is your boss, is an essential skill for survival in business. Interviews with those who regularly have angry outbursts at work as well as those who have to work with them will bring a crucial new level of understanding. Just like Pixar's 2015 box office hit *Inside Out*, there is a time where anger and other emotions need to run the show, but you need to know just how to harness yours and those of others. This chapter also explores how you can reflect on what is causing your reactions as well as how to understand it, articulate it, and use it at the right time and in the right place.

CHAPTER TOPICS

- Strengthening Your Zone of Resilience
- How to Let Anger Run the Show
- Venting or Complaining?
- Opening the Door to Talking About Emotions
- When You Say the Wrong Thing
- Top Ten Communication Mistakes

- Naming Your Emotions
- Judging Your Judgmentalism
- Harnessing the Power of Positive Emotions
- Becoming Imperturbable

"Let me be clear, I don't do fluffy!**"**

I hope you won't decide to skip this chapter thinking that it will be all talk about fluffy esoteric nonsense with no bearing on anything of significance. I promise: I don't do fluffy.

It is common for executives, leaders, or even most adults to find it challenging to name and talk about their emotions beyond positive ones. If that has not been part of your vocabulary, it may require some additional reflection time. It is why I provide the Emotions Word Circle in Figure 7.1 to give you words to help you describe what you are experiencing.

FIGURE 7.1   Emotions Word Circle

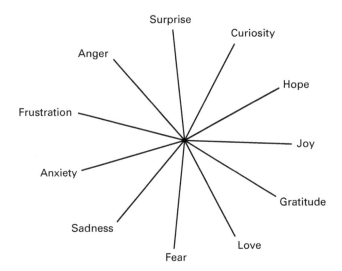

As you read the Emotions Word Circle, you may find you have a reaction to some of the emotions, and you may be drawn to others. In this chapter we will explore the most explosive emotions and those for which you need specific Words That Work to understand and manage through.

Strengthening Your Zone of Resilience

My brilliant therapist, Dr. Susan Reedy, taught me about the zone of resilience. She drew it on a pad, but I like to explain it physically, because I usually tell this story from the stage when speaking, so let me explain. Put your arms horizontally in front of your face on top of each other. Now open them up a few inches. The gap between your two arms is the zone of resilience. Your mood will bounce between those zones quite happily, if you imagine a wavy line bouncing between your arms moving left to right. That is your emotions changing as you go through your day. Not all your emotions can stay within that zone of resilience. An event may provoke a reaction that causes your emotions to push you out the top of your resilience zone—a customer didn't sign the big deal you expected, or your pitch for a new strategy investment was rejected by the CFO, or someone cut you off in the parking lot and nearly hit your car. Any of those incidents could trigger a response where you no longer feel in control. That can lead to a manifestation of anger as we stereotypically expect to see it, with raised voices, exaggerated hand gestures, and cutting remarks, or it can show up through passive-aggressive or sarcastic comments instead.

I am not a trained psychologist but I do know where the boundaries lie, and where support and counseling is required by those trained in the profession. But many of us simply need some practical communication tips that help with noticing when it may occur, and what to do once you have busted right out of your zone. Anger is the least discussed emotion in the workplace, so we'll address that first.

How to Let Anger Run the Show

The least talked about emotion may be your most untapped opportunity. Anger really can be that powerful. Unfortunately, the ostrich effect in difficult situations leaves no room for exploration. Burying your head in the sand is not helpful. Instead, seek to understand and unpack what provokes you, causes you to bust out of your zone of resilience and feel angry. Most of us can't hear advice in the heat of the moment, so I hope next time you can remember to try this:

> **"**Be curious when you are furious.**"**

Curiosity is heightened when the unexpected happens. I love to share ideas and lessons in the most unexpected ways and in the most unusual places; I enjoy positively provoking people to think differently. I would never have thought I would advise thousands of leaders around the world to watch a Pixar movie, but indeed I have. Disney-owned Pixar released a movie called *Inside Out* about a girl named Riley who reluctantly moved cities as a teenager. The viewer sees her life through the lens of her emotions that are controlling her brain. I wrote about my lessons from that movie in my *Inc. Magazine* column at the time and it was one of the top-read articles that month.

In the movie, Anger is characterized as a short, red, shouting man who regularly has steam coming out of his ears. He reminded me of my first store manager as an eighteen-year-old management trainee in British store group House of Fraser. He was one of the smartest leaders I ever worked for, as well as being caring. He paid attention to even us junior trainees, but he would regularly bust out of his zone. Looking back, I can see what his triggers were: not taking care of our customers, appearing like you didn't care about your job, and appearing to not give your job your full effort. All three of those came to a head one afternoon when my pager went off and I had to call his office. "Valerie, get this girl out of my store NOW!" he screamed over the phone. I couldn't get him to explain any more details as he was so mad. He was angry because one of the sales team was chatting with friends and not being attentive to customers. He couldn't even talk to her, so he called me to complain and deal with the situation.

Research from UC Berkeley[1] suggests that expressing anger can lead to more successful negotiations in life and at work. Psychologist John Riskind created a useful speedometer that lets you categorize the various levels of your anger and provides different advice on how to handle each speed. Just like the movie, anger sometimes needs to run the show.

Venting or Complaining?

It never ceases to amaze me how the advice I learn at work helps me in my whole life and vice versa. Lisa Damour came to my daughters' school to talk about her brilliant book *Untangled: Guiding teenage girls through the seven transitions into adulthood* (I highly recommend it). In the book she stopped me cold when she described the difference between venting and complaining:

Venting means you are just letting off steam. You are not looking for advice, a solution, or feedback, just an open ear and perhaps a touch of empathy.

Complaining means you are seeking advice. You want help thinking through how to deal with what you are sharing. You don't want sympathy, you want solutions.

If you haven't heard this nuance about complaining, don't you find it so incredibly insightful? Next time someone is sharing a situation with you, try this powerful question:

"Do you want help with that, or do you just need to vent?**"**

Think back to all the angry interactions you have experienced: did you know if they were venting or complaining? Perhaps you tried to offer advice but they just wanted to vent. Or maybe they wanted options and solutions, but you only comforted them.

This is how you harness the power of your anger, or the anger you are experiencing in others. The crossover for your whole life is there too. I learned the nuance of these definitions two years ago. Since then, I must have saved hundreds of hours by asking my husband if he is venting or complaining; 95 percent of the time he is simply venting. I dare not calculate how many hours I previously wasted or how much I frustrated him in my attempts to help when he was simply venting! The power of two simple words potentially with similar meanings but which unlock infinite ways to communicate more clearly.

This is a crucial question I include in the Words That Work vocabulary guide when I work with executive teams. Try asking the next person who appears angry:

> **"**Are you venting and want me
> to listen, or complaining and want help?**"**

To return to your zone of resilience, that zone can increase or it can shrink, depending on what you are dealing with at the time. The good news is you can train it to get bigger. Put your arms back up to create the zone, and you can widen them so the peaks and troughs of your emotions can be higher and lower and you don't bust out of your zone.

In 2020 and 2021 some of the most requested themes for my keynotes and workshops were communication and unlocking cross-group results. The reason for this was that the pandemic collectively reduced many people's resilience zones—what they could tolerate in those years suddenly became more difficult to handle.

Anger pushes you out of the top of your resilience zone. If you fall out of the bottom of your zone, that is where your sadness kicks in, and your ability to hold it together diminishes and the tears may fall.

Victor Meldrew is a humorous character on the British television show *One Foot in the Grave*. He epitomizes the grumpy old miserable British retiree who sees the bad and the misery in every situation. Are you imagining the Victor Meldrews you know in your life?

There are three leaders I work with who I always know will mention difficult situations that are happening to them in their first several comments to me whenever we speak—pointing out others' mistakes, bemoaning the futility of any new initiatives, or generally lacking any hope or optimism. Their teams don't want them to be fake-nice, but relentless negativity does get exhausting. I wondered if they knew or if anyone had ever pointed it out to them. So I tested it out by saying:

> **"**I've noticed a pattern: you notice what you don't like, but not what you do.**"**

As I gave each leader that feedback individually, all three were completely surprised; no one had ever pointed it out. They also got a bonus education on British 1980s sitcoms and who Victor Meldrew was. Each came back to me the following week saying they had watched one of the shows and could see why I made that connection! It isn't hard to find Victors in many companies. Most do it with a positive spin, with the intent to improve and learn from mistakes, not to take an "ain't-it-awful" approach where misery loves company and Eeyore likes to be with other Eeyores.

As I gave those executives this feedback, I was then quiet. Silence is important when you make observations such as this one. Of course, it is easier to fill the void, explain away your comment, or layer on multiple comments when you need the equivalent of the white space on the page around what you say by way of silence. It is the same reason why, when writing this book, I explained to my editor at Kogan Page the importance of the giant "quotation marks" around the Words That Work—because it is like the dramatic pause if I was speaking. The white space draws your eyes to the words, and the words are important, just as silence is important when you are having conversations that are not typical. If you want to explore in more detail the power of white space when communicating then I highly recommend reading *The Poet X*.[2] It was assigned reading for my thirteen-year-old and as soon as I had submitted the first draft of the manuscript for this book to my publisher, I wanted to escape and read something completely unique. As I flicked through the book I was captivated. The written words were like a form of art; the way the story was told visually was incredible. There was a point where ants on a page were being described

and   the   words
                       on   the
page   appeared   like   ants
        and   it   just
visually   showed   the   words

This form of poetry is called concrete poetry, where the shape of the poetry is just as important as the message itself.

As you consider the emotions that you want to evoke with the words that you use, consider how you can use the white space on the page to deliver your message in unique ways.

Imagine receiving this message in an email:

> **"You were fantastic in that meeting!"**

Nothing more, no explanation, no details, no justification, no buts, no caveats, no perhaps do this better. Just one simple line of praise. What emotions would that trigger for you? Likely ones that are positive, removing any self-doubt and lifting your confidence. Sometimes fewer words are more important than being verbose.

Opening the Door to Talking About Emotions

If this was a workshop this would be the point in time when about a quarter of you stand up and go and get a cup of coffee, take a call, or take a comfort break. Of course I can see the pattern; after decades of running events around the world, when it comes to the interaction part of any conversation at an event, the result is predictable. The reason I know this is because when I am in the audience, I may well be one of the restless and unwilling! So, with my low tolerance for fluff and unsubstantiated reflection, I will share a method that I have seen to be effective in starting conversations where emotions are discussed. In your next meeting, at the start, ask the following:

> **"**Take a minute and write down
> three emotions that are present with you.**"**

If you get a confused reaction, you can explain not to worry about the words they use, but just to write down the first three emotions that come to mind as they pause and think about where they are, right here, right now. Three emotions. They can stop at two or even one if they wish. You may be surprised by what gets shared.

When You Say the Wrong Thing

> **"**I wish I could take that back!**"**

Have you ever wanted to reach for the words that just left your mouth and pull them back inside? I will never forget Daryll's face as soon as he had finished his sentence. It was in front of an audience of twenty-two people around a U-shaped table in the executive conference room at his company's New York headquarters. I watched the room react, from the single raised eyebrow to the slow closing of another's eyes to the instant reaction of one of them clasping a hand in front of their own mouth as though they had uttered those words. Afterward Daryll shared with me how his stomach had done several flips in quick succession as he opened his mouth to speak again. What he said and did next could mean the difference between a funded new strategy with unanimous support, or a mediocre reaction, a middle-of-the-road bonus, or a blocked strategy and months or years of recovery.

For everyone who has had one of those stomach-flipping moments, the rest of this chapter explores when words don't work, and what to do if you happen to make one of the top ten communication mistakes explained next.

Top Ten Communication Mistakes

1 Being passive-aggressive

2 Making personal attacks

3 Offering ungrounded opinions

4 Making unexplained in-jokes

5 Using sarcasm

6 Covering up the truth

7 Radio silence

8 Using corporate buzz words

9 Context-sensitive misuse of time

10 Excessively, repetitively, ridiculously, never able to stop, can't end when you have made your point, tire people out to the point of frustration by being verbose

Before I go on to explain why these are such bad mistakes and what to do when you encounter them, take a look at the top ten list again and note which are your top three pet peeves. Now look for a second time and note which three are most prevalent within your team. Now look at the list one last time and note which you are most susceptible to.

Top three annoyances:

1

2

3

Top three most prevalent:

1

2

3

Top three I am most prone to:

1

2

3

You can run this as an exercise at the start of your next team meeting and compare notes. It is a fascinating way to open up truth telling and establish company or team norms for what is okay and what drives people to distraction with how we communicate together.

Overcoming the Top Ten Communication Mistakes

1. BEING PASSIVE-AGGRESSIVE

Indirectly commenting on an issue or concern shows aggression in a roundabout way that can trigger many negative emotions. When encountering a passive-aggressive comment many withdraw, become silent or bluster a defensive response. Instead, try these three retorts:

"Why don't you share what you are really concerned about?"

"You sound frustrated, what is behind that?"

"Is your concern A or B or something else?"

2. MAKING PERSONAL ATTACKS

Ever feel like you are back at school when in fact you are still at work? I am constantly amazed at some of the commentary I hear leaders share about their peers, bosses, and colleagues. When you hear commentary about someone personally, how easy is it for you to proverbially put your fingers in your ears and say "lalala I don't want to hear this personal attack"? It isn't easy to stop the bickering and gossip, but it only stops when people stop listening to it. When you hear someone attacking another colleague personally, use one of these three responses to challenge and end the personal criticism:

> **"**Is that feedback you have shared with them directly? Perhaps start there?**"**

> **"**Is your concern with them personally, or the project they are working on?**"**

> **"**That's harsh, should you really be sharing that with us? **"**

3. OFFERING UNGROUNDED OPINIONS

Fact and opinion can easily get blurred, causing communication confusion if you don't challenge unfounded opinions. The louder and bolder you communicate, the more you can convince an audience that your opinion is fact when the opposite is true. There are two important differentiators to make. First, if you are sharing your opinion, introduce it as just that and what you are basing your opinion on:

> **"**Here's what I have found from my time here...**"**

> **"**I've formed this opinion based on the last three projects...**"**

Second, if you want to challenge someone else's ungrounded opinion, try these questions:

> **"**How did you reach that conclusion?**"**

> **"**What led you to form that point of view?**"**

> **"**Is that based on what you have observed here or elsewhere?**"**

4. MAKING UNEXPLAINED IN-JOKES

Shared experiences bond teams, but there is a fine line between recounting great memories and creating exclusive in-jokes only a few understand or can relate to. This one is simple to overcome: be aware of your audience when sharing funny memories and don't do it on company conference calls, in meetings, or with those who don't understand the context. If you hear an in-joke you don't understand, for the benefit of everyone who isn't in the in-club, simply say:

"That sounds funny, what did I miss?"

5. USING SARCASM

When I moved from England to Seattle when I worked at Microsoft, this was the biggest cultural shock I had not truly appreciated until I tried unsuccessfully to make typically British sarcastic comments at the most inopportune moments. There is both a company and country cultural tolerance for sarcasm, and frankly everyone needs to be taught during their onboarding just the precise level of sarcasm that is typical. If in doubt simply don't use it. Which for a British leader working in the US for the first time is far easier to say than actually to change habits and do!

6. COVERING UP THE TRUTH

While I covered this in depth in Chapter 1, hiding the truth or creating the illusion of inclusion when you are not sharing the full details triggers anxiety, fear, and frustration among your team and peers. If you suspect others may not be sharing the full facts, try asking these questions:

"I get the sense there may be more to understand here..."

"Is there additional context or information that you can share?"

"What am I missing?"

7. RADIO SILENCE

This is the most deceptive communication mistake to make because it triggers the most creative and inventive versions of the truth for those on the receiving end of the deafening silence. Often those versions of the truth are completely disconnected from reality and the simple truth is often that the communicator is at their own version of overwhelm and just hasn't had the time or focus to respond. This triggers fear, doubt, frustration, and a sense that their question, query, or report is not of any importance. If you are perpetually guilty of radio silence, perhaps try focusing on the root cause, which is often a lack of organization or prioritization, or even a fear of giving bad news or doubting your own judgement. You may already know that you may need extra time, or simply need to get better at acknowledging incoming work, questions, or queries. Consider this at the start and during those moments that typically trigger your radio silence.

When first received:

"Received, I may need a few days, I'll reply by Friday.**"**

"Received, I have a few competing priorities, I will reply by next week.**"**

"Thanks for your questions, let's schedule a call next week.**"**

If it is taking longer than expected:

"I promised to get back to you by ____ but I need a few more days.**"**

"Sorry for the delay, you will hear from me by...**"**

"I can answer your first question, but let's discuss the others on...**"**

If you are on the receiving end of radio silence, one of these three phrases will prompt a response:

"Can you let me know when I can expect to hear back from you?"

"I'd love to hear from you by x date because..."

"I'd love to hear from you by x date, otherwise I will take this action..."

If the echo of silence continues, as a last resort use:

"It is unusual to not hear back, can you let me know that you are ok?"

8. USING CORPORATE BUZZ WORDS

The most ridiculed words that don't work are the corporate buzz words that sprout up in unexpected places like weeds in a garden. Nobody wants them and they are impossible to get rid of. But they multiply when you are not looking. When I worked at Microsoft and they relocated me from England to Seattle, there was one Four Tops song that stuck in my head every day; I couldn't help but silently sing it every time someone asked to "reach out" rather than call or email.

I remember working at British department store House of Fraser back in the 1990s and experiencing my first-ever management consultant as a twenty-something manager trying to eagerly prove myself. I was part of a national project to improve the sales and profit per square foot across fifty-two department stores around the UK. I started working with a group of consultants for the first time and was in shock at the amount of buzz words, weird catchphrases, and incomprehensible references that were made to describe the simplest activities.

What are the most annoying buzz words that you despise? I am always amused to hear the latest words that have been adopted for well-intended impact when amusement is all that occurs. My worst top three are:

- I'll circle back with you later.
- Let's double click on this topic.
- You need to take this offline.

You might be wondering if corporate buzz words are really that harmful but they just increase the chances of misinterpretation and confusion. The fastest way to reduce or eliminate such jargon is with humor. Ask your team what are common buzz words in your company and how they interpret them. Decide which you want to keep and which you want to root out from your corporate vocabulary. If you are ever confused, simply repeat the buzz word and ask:

"What does that mean to you?"

9. CONTEXT-SENSITIVE MISUSE OF TIME

Watch how your meetings typically start. Is there socialization, informal conversations, catching up on personal news, or is it straight down to business? The greatest emotional reactions I see in meetings are when there is a mismatch of behavior and expectations for how time is used. I'll never forget Michael's bumpy start joining a company on their executive team I worked with. Every meeting, Michael started by commenting on sports news, his weekend plans, or asking about someone's pet. What Michael had failed to read was the context-sensitive nature of conversations with the executive team. Even when the company had missed its sales targets and had a technology failure, the social chit chat prevailed. After a couple of weeks, I asked Michael to notice the pattern of communication at the start of every meeting by noting on his pad who started the conversations, who spoke about business or personal topics. Until this reflection time, Michael hadn't picked up on the social communication cues for this executive team and failed to notice he was operating as an anomaly in his social conversations, triggering frustration and anger in his peers, especially when the company wasn't performing.

10. EXCESSIVELY, REPETITIVELY, RIDICULOUSLY, NEVER ABLE TO STOP, CAN'T END WHEN YOU HAVE MADE YOUR POINT, TIRE PEOPLE OUT TO THE POINT OF FRUSTRATION BY BEING VERBOSE

I'll keep this advice short, because:

"Why use a paragraph when a sentence will do?"

"Why use a sentence when one word will do?"

"Why use one word when silence will do?"

Naming Your Emotions

When you name your emotions, it grounds you in noticing them rather than being washed away by them. One executive I worked with used to pound his fist when he spoke during the quarterly business reviews, sometimes ex-act-ly-in-time-to-the-words-he-said. His outbursts reverberated throughout the meetings and people feared being in those business reviews with him, nervously anticipating his next explosion. He was oblivious that he was expressing himself that way, and in the following quarterly business review he started to pound his fist, but on the second thump he said:

"I am frustrated with myself that I missed the sales goals again."

This was not what anyone was expecting; he then went on to say:

"Please point out when I pound the table, I don't always notice!"

Not only did he stop the behavior that others perceived as angry and intimidating, he showed a vulnerable side, sharing that he didn't know he pounded the table and he was disappointed in himself that he was missing his sales numbers.

Judging Your Judgmentalism

When we pass judgment, we attach labels to others' behavior. They are too slow. They are not strategic. They are always angry.

If you find yourself struggling to be empathetic, think for a moment about someone who annoys you greatly. Now rethink your opinion of them, showing them the greatest amount of grace. Imagine a scenario where they need your empathy, not judgment. Let go of the story you tell yourself when you judge them. Let go of the power they have over your time and headspace.

Harnessing the Power of Positive Emotions

Don't forget that loving your emotions also involves loving your positive emotions. As a leader, your ability to instill hope, joy, and curiosity will create a differentiator for your company. You can creatively achieve this through art. When womenswear retailer francesca's successfully moved from public company to private equity ownership, I wanted to give a gift that symbolized the year they had been through refinancing and restricting their company. I knew I wanted to incorporate a phoenix, but it needed to be an everlasting gift. My hyper-focused brain pays off in these situations because I went down a very long, deep, endless Google search tunnel, and eventually discovered glass paperweights with an ornate phoenix inside, from the Caithness Glass factory in Scotland. Each member of the management team received one, and they became much talked about in the company's all-hands and strategy planning sessions. Each leader talked about what the francesca's phoenix meant for them, the journey they had personally been on when the company was up for sale and decided to go through the Chapter 11 restructuring process. It became a mascot, an emblem everyone could rally around. It served as a spark of hope. CEO Andrew Clarke's definition of it was particularly powerful at the first company all-hands after the sale of the company:

> This is a phoenix, rising from the flames. It truly represents francesca's emerging from all the challenges we have overcome in the last ten months, and I want to thank you all for the support and dedication to allow us to be here today. A phoenix is the ultimate symbol of strength, renewal, transformation, and passion. I am here to let you know today that following our auction process, we get to continue on our journey together as a fran family.

What art or emblems could you adopt?

Becoming Imperturbable

As you reflect on your understanding of your emotions, use Figure 7.2 to take a snapshot of what you have discovered. Consider it an emotions

FIGURE 7.2 Loving Your Emotions

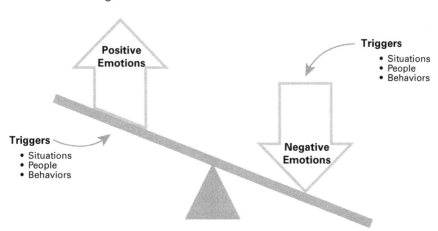

audit of what lifts you up and what drags you down. Your strength and your untapped opportunity lie in becoming imperturbable, so that others' actions or emotions do not knock you off course. This may vary based on the time of year, level of growth or innovation, or even when you have a board meeting pending, which we go on to explore next.

Endnotes

1 Kashdan, T and Biswas-Diener, R (2014) The right way to get angry, *Greater Good*, https://greatergood.berkeley.edu/article/item/the_right_way_to_get_angry (archived at https://perma.cc/LUY8-Y5RM)

2 Acevedo, E (2018) *The Poet X*, Harper Teen

08

Taking the Boredom Out
of Your Board of Directors

Successful CEOs turn board relationships upside down. Instead of presenting to, responding to, and answering to their board of directors, they actively lead them. A successful CEO knows just how to unlock the capability and capacity of their board to make them exemplary. Customer spending, channels for marketing, and entire industries can change overnight. The challenge is determining whether your board is succeeding. Results alone don't tell the full story; in fact, results can obscure the true issues that may be holding the company back. This chapter explores the crucial questions to ask your board, tools to evaluate your board, and lessons from successful CEOs and their boards.

CHAPTER TOPICS

- Fueling Your Powerful Board

- Ten Steps to Cultivating a Relationship with Your Board

- Four Top Challenges of Working with a Board

- Recognizing Success

Fueling Your Powerful Board

Imagine having an inner circle of advisors who complement your skills, have a vested interest in your success, and bring with them an incredible network of business opportunities. That is the power of a powerful board. As CEO, it is easy to feel subservient to your board; in fact, the board effectively works for you, to support you and grow the business.

The first step to building a powerful board is selecting the right CEO to build the board around. Next, the board has to galvanize across six key areas in this order.

Step One: Clarity of Exit

A board's actions will vary greatly depending on whether the company is headed toward an IPO versus a longer-term growth play. If only part of the board is aware of the ultimate exit plan, your strategies will be futile and investments wasted because the speed and sequence of your products, expansion, and acquisition plans will vary greatly. The dynamics of a public versus a private board obviously vary greatly, but the intent and importance of these areas remain equally as high. The consequences of not following them may have broader repercussions for a public board. Regardless of ownership status, the whole board needs to be able to consistently say:

> **"**Here is our exit plan and likely time window.**"**

Step Two: Align Strategy

There is often healthy tension between a CEO and their board regarding their degree of involvement in the creation and implementation of strategy. Chapter 11 outlines the Right Spot, Right Moment framework to help everyone set the right boundaries. When I have worked with boards which have prolific players, they bring unique insight about how to set the strategic direction and the choices on how to get there. As you sit through your board meetings, evaluate the mix of time that the board spends on tactics versus strategies. What time horizon is the discussion referring to? The next six months or the next three years? You may need to remind everyone:

"Let's elevate from the tactics. I really want your advice on..."

WORDS THAT WORK DECONSTRUCTION

- Did you wince when you read those words I suggested saying to your board? Whenever I suggest this to leaders, about 50 percent physically screw up their faces and ask me if I really mean it.

- What I am proposing here is a PIVOT. It is a way of showing someone a different topic to focus on that is more relevant to their role AND gets them out of the details of your business.

- Note that the first five words are all positive. It would have been easy to say, "Let's not get stuck in the details...," but there are three potential negative words in that phrase. Negative words do not work. If you deliver your feedback through a positive lens, it is easier for the receiver to accept it and agree.

Step Three: Introduce Accelerators

You expect your board members to bring idea accelerators to every strategic conversation. Here's a test. Create a scoring mechanism for your next board meeting. List all the board members down the left-hand column of a page in your notebook; now, each time a board member makes a suggestion or provides insight, make a checkmark next to their name and note what the suggestion was. I have suggested this to many CEOs as I have helped them prepare their board presentations, and they come back with such fascinating insights—from not realizing how many ideas and acceleration points some board members make that get lost in the group dynamic, to being shocked at the resounding silence from some board members on their contributions to growing the business. This is where the mindset shift occurs, whether the CEO is newly appointed and eager to please and perform in front of their board, or a seasoned veteran who can summon history and comparisons. (Note: much of this chapter will have stories from anonymous sources, because that way you get far more detail and insight than if a quote has been through the board and company corporate PR approvals process!)

Step Four: Talent Connectors

Here is a perfect question to ask your board member:

"Who do you know in the ... space?"

I was coaching a CEO who would be interviewing a potential board member, and I gave him that advice. He shared the company's five-year strategy, then he asked her three versions of the "who do you know" question to test how strong a talent connector she could be on the board. This question also tests the altitude of a board member's network. As explained in Chapter 3, it is easy for anyone's network to become dehydrated, stagnant, and set at the incorrect seniority level. Powerful board members need to have connections at the CEO, reporting to the CEO, board member, or investor level. I always say the use of a headhunter for an executive hire is a leading indicator that the CEO and board have one of two challenges: either a dehydrated network or an invisible reputation. Otherwise they would have a flood of potential candidates through referrals in their network and spontaneous outreach.

Step Five: Reputation Amplifiers

The days of men in suits carrying briefcases into board meetings with paper briefings and minutes might be a throwback to my first board meetings in London a couple of decades ago, but sometimes when I meet board members I do feel like some could be stuck in a time warp. Today, founders, CEOs, and investors tend to have a virtual presence and online reputation. It is how you tell your story, strengthen your message, reach new audiences, and use your platform to amplify the *raison d'être* and reputation of your company. Yet when I do an online search on many board members, I cannot find them: they don't exist on social networks, and some are blindly happy to be anonymous. That just doesn't cut it today.

Take Arlan Hamilton, for instance. She uses her voice for those who don't have a voice, amplifying the companies she invests in and the boards she sits on. It helps that she wrote a brilliant best-selling book, *It's About Damn Time: How to turn being underestimated into your greatest advantage.* Hamilton has invested $5 million in 100 companies, and invests in founders who identify as women, people of color, or LGBTQ+. Her story is mind-blowing: she went from being homeless in the San Francisco airport to breaking into the white-boys-VC club of Silicon Valley. Most recently she set up a scholarship for Oxford University in the UK, for those of Black African and Caribbean heritage. Today, Mark Cuban, investor on ABC's *Shark Tank,* is one of her mentors, and she is continuing to expand her impact. She was the first investor in Roots Dolls, a company that creates multicultural children's toys.[1] Hamilton also launched a crowdfunding VC fund for underrepresented founders that raised over $3.1 million in the first twenty-four hours, which enthralled me so much I invested in the fund myself. Does that set the benchmark for what a reputation amplifier can do as they join your board?

My favorite quote from Hamilton is relevant for every board member and aspiring board member:

"Be yourself so the people looking for you can find you.**"**

These wise words were proven when francesca's CEO Andrew Clarke was interviewed by CNBC as part of their partnership with the Pride initiative. Clarke is a rare publicly gay CEO, and he shared his story externally for the first time in a video interview for 2021 Pride month. This interview led to an outpouring of support from around the world, thanking Clarke for telling his story and saying how inspiring it was for others who could relate.

Step Six: Governance Discipline

Perhaps the least exciting area the board needs to galvanize around is the discipline of governance. It's a critical one, however. The disastrous public examples of oversight, whistleblowing, and accountability with Boeing, Wells Fargo, and WeWork are good reminders that this area requires dedicated attention. The dynamic between a private board and the founder has always been shrouded in tension. Bill Gurley of the venture capital firm Benchmark told *The Wall Street Journal* that Silicon Valley is such a competitive VC market that "too many people" worry about "whether they have a buddy-buddy relationship with the founder."[2] This may allude to the challenges with WeWork; at the time of the interview Benchmark was the second-largest shareholder.

These six steps to a powerful board are represented in the Fueling Your Powerful Board tool in Figure 8.1. At the heart is the CEO, surrounded by the board, with the fuel, or fire, underneath coming from the behaviors and active engagement—all of which produces exemplary results.

FIGURE 8.1   Fueling Your Powerful Board

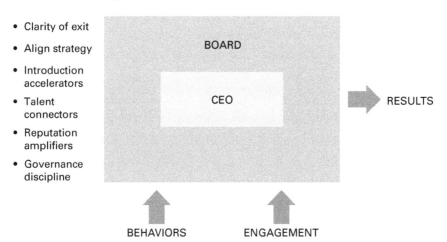

- Clarity of exit
- Align strategy
- Introduction accelerators
- Talent connectors
- Reputation amplifiers
- Governance discipline

BOARD

CEO

RESULTS

BEHAVIORS   ENGAGEMENT

Chairman Tim Baskerville made an intentional appointment of Meredith Amdur to the board of business intelligence company Wanted Analytics. Five years later he further validated that he had made the right decision when Amdur was appointed CEO. He knew that he needed a longer-term successor for the incumbent CEO. With a background at Direct TV, Microsoft, Variety, and Deloitte, executive Amdur was a strong choice. Five years later, after she had immersed herself in the business and played an active role in the company's strategic planning process, Amdur further proved Baskerville made the right choice when after three months the stock price rose 37 percent. A year later Amdur positioned the company for a successful sale to Gartner-owned CEB at a remarkable premium price.

Amdur was able to exemplify the behaviors required to fuel the powerful board. In our work together, Amdur prepared for her transition from board member to CEO, to creating the perfect launch plan—which you can find in Chapter 10—and supporting her external investor and media relations as she created new revenue streams and retained key talent. You can follow these rapid 10 steps to building your relationships with your board, but don't forget to watch out for the four top challenges before you start to recognize your success.

Ten Steps to Cultivating a Relationship with Your Board

1 Reflect and assess your exemplary board.

2 Review your network analysis.

3 Upgrade to an enviable inner circle for advice.

4 Identify which one-on-one relationships need investment.

5 Understand the value, expertise, and power of each board member.

6 Create agreement for how and where your board is involved.

7 Share your intentions and thoughts in your communication.

8 Focus on three things you will improve in the next three months.

9 Find an advisor who observes you and works on specific goals.

10 Join the National Association of Corporate Directors or Institute of Directors for your own development.

Four Top Challenges of Working with a Board

- Giving the CEO the freedom to lead.
- Active involvement vs observers from one quarter to the next.
- Balance of power in founder-led companies.
- Resolving conflict when your interactions are sporadic.

Recognizing Success

"The board just agreed to everything I asked for, Val! My three-year strategy, my technology investment, my marketing strategy, and who I need to hire and fire."

That is what a CEO called to tell me on day forty-two of taking the helm of a NASDAQ company. In our work together his preparation had been meticulous. He created an innovative strategy and bold financial plan, but the crucial preparation occurred in the scripts that he planned. The precise language was choreographed like a theatre production for his pre-calls with each board member and during the actual board meeting. The results? Decisions made, investments approved, strategies blessed, and executive moves endorsed, all in record time, with the board having increased confidence in his ability and giving him more freedom for future decisions. A month later he reported his first quarterly earnings as CEO, and the stock price more than doubled!

Your board can play a crucial role in the external reputation of the company, with intentional focus on your investor and media interactions, which the next chapter explores.

Endnotes

1 http://healthyrootsdolls.com (archived at https://perma.cc/C5US-TPXA)

2 Winkler, R (2019) For WeWork investor Benchmark, a struggle to balance board duties with founder support, *Wall Street Journal*, https://www.wsj.com/articles/for-wework-investor-benchmark-a-struggle-to-balance-board-duties-with-founder-support-11569341467 (archived at https://perma.cc/LUU6-35HS)

09

Turning Investor and Media Interactions to Your Advantage

Managing your Wall Street, investor or City relationships as well as media relations should be a 365-day priority. It's not just for earnings call week, when you need to fundraise, launch a new product, or announce an acquisition. It needs to happen in parallel to your internal communications. This chapter provides the inspiration CEOs and leaders need prior to stepping on the external stage. You will learn the right preparation, questions, and insider tips to make your media interviews, earnings calls, investor meetings, and fundraising campaigns go without a hiccup.

CHAPTER TOPICS

- The CEO Communications Dilemma
- The Myths and Realities of External Communications
- Exemplary Executive Communication
- Communication Lessons from TV Shows
- The Video Review Everyone Loves to Hate

The CEO Communications Dilemma

There are two extremes of a continuum for CEOs when communicating internally, with investors, and with the media: those who adore it and those who avoid it at all costs.

Imagine for a moment that there is a stack of cards on a table. Each card holds a topic that could be about any aspect of your business. You now have to pick a card from the stack and immediately talk about that topic for five minutes without stopping. Let's pause for a moment to consider, how do you feel about that?

Your reaction may range from "bring it on" to "hmmm, ok if I must," or even "that sounds terrible, I need more preparation!" You may also have more questions before giving your answer, wanting to know who would be in the audience, would this be internal to your company or external, the size of the audience, a small group or your whole company, or an external conference, or even a small group of CEOs you have known for the last ten years.

I walk you through this theoretical game as I do when I start working with an executive on increasing their communication impact because it helps us understand where you have strength and confidence, and where you have not yet mastered this expertise.

While it is unlikely you will have to play the random topic card game, it does help you put yourself in certain communication scenarios and consider what it is you dislike most about those situations. Let's first consider all of the possible scenarios where you have to be on stage as a CEO.

You can use the Executive Communications Evaluation in Figure 9.1 to reflect on the most common scenarios where the spotlight is on you as a CEO or executive representing your company. For each of the seven internal and eight external communication events, rate along the scale how much you adore doing them vs trying to avoid them—and be a truth teller in your evaluation.

As you compare the first seven with the last eight, what do you see? I often find that CEOs and executives are far more comfortable with the internal communications than the external. If you have areas where you are avoiding rather than adoring, turn back to Chapter 4

FIGURE 9.1   Executive Communications Evaluation

ADORE	AVOID
INTERNAL	Writing company updates
	Writing business board reports
	Creating visual deck presentations
	All-company meetings
	Free-flowing Q+A sessions
	Small group discussions
	1–1s

EXTERNAL	1–1 discussions in private
	Investor days
	Conference panels
	Conference fireside chats
	Conference keynotes
	TV interviews
	Print interviews
	Podcast interviews

Plot which communications you adore or avoid

to learn valuable tips and ideas for strengthening your internal communications. We will dive further into how to learn to adore your external communications opportunities next.

The Myths and Realities of External Communications

Don't discount this whole chapter as something you don't need to do because you are a private company, because your owners are reluctant to be in the media, because you don't have an ego so don't need to be appearing on TV and at conferences. Let's listen to our contrarians on this topic and dispel a few external communications myths.

Myth One: Only CEOs with Big Egos Spend Time in the Media

Despite how it may appear if you watch CNBC's business news show *Squawk Box*, or other stations such as Bloomberg TV, not all CEOs who appear in the media are attention seeking and PR hungry. Quite the opposite, as those who do appear have intentionally planned where and when they want to get their message across to which audiences. The greatest secret to this is the upside that your own employees get to see their company and leaders in the press, being interviewed and featured at conferences, which increases their confidence in their employer and allows them to hear key messages from external sources.

"External communications are the fastest way to reach your employees."

Myth Two: Only Public Companies Need External Communications

While companies have quarterly earnings cycles that drive their key messages, there are more reasons to communicate to your investors and the media than the reaction of the market to your results. The most overlooked one is your ability to attract key talent to your company. If you had to choose between two job offers where all was equal, but one company had significant evidence of its success through interviews, videos, and media reports, most candidates would choose the company that has greater external recognition. The balance of power for hiring is in the hands of candidates; companies need to create their virtual reputation and evidence of success far more now than in years gone by.

Myth Three: You Need Big News to Appear in the News

Not all news has to be big news. Investors, media, communities want to hear real-life stories that they can relate to, whether it is a feel-good story where your company is supporting a local philanthropic cause, an employee-focused story of success, or you are changing direction with the products and services you are offering your customers. All of those are worthy of updates and a spotlight for your investors and the media.

Myth Four: My Investors Only Want to Communicate Privately

I have witnessed even the most discreet and off-the-grid investors delight in the external media that their companies have received. The key is to choose your outlets and stories intentionally and be sure that the messages you are sharing are at the right pace with what your investors want known to the outside world at this point in time. It is too easy to prematurely communicate success, or to overtly reveal a new strategic direction that might tip your competitors' hand, so preparation is crucial, but that doesn't mean radio silence is the only option.

Myth Five: Media and Investor Relationships are Incredibly Distracting

While this focus does not come without dedicating time to it, the return on investment is clear. Your ability to reach new strategic partners, vendors, or future investors is reliant on how you tell your story externally. The trick to not entering the external communications black hole where your time disappears is to have the right communications and public relations expertise available to you.

Now we have dispelled the myths, and you know which communication elements you adore and avoid, let us look at the reasons why CEOs avoid or adore communicating externally and what you can do about it.

Exemplary Executive Communication

Remember your last media interview? How did you feel as the camera panned to you and you started speaking? Did you feel in control, confident of your lines and excited to share your message? Or perhaps you were running between back-to-back meetings, hadn't had time to clear your head or review your script? Have you ever felt like a talking head where you can't connect to the words that are falling from your lips that someone else wrote for you and you are wondering exactly what you will say next?

There are three crucial parts to Exemplary Executive Communication, and the impact of those is demonstrated in Figure 9.2.

FIGURE 9.2 Exemplary Executive Communication

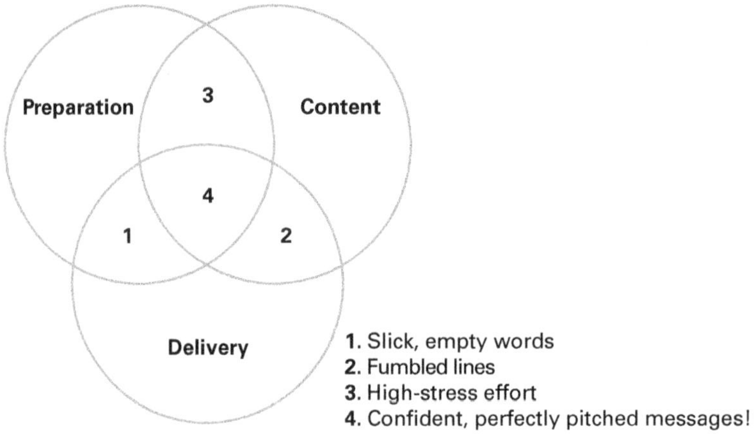
Preparation
3
Content
4
1
2
Delivery
1. Slick, empty words
2. Fumbled lines
3. High-stress effort
4. Confident, perfectly pitched messages!

- **Preparation:** Your preparation needs to be done at a pace you are comfortable with. Some CEOs like to write their own talking points and scripts, then let someone else finesse and edit them. Others prefer to give a verbal download and let their communications guru craft the soundbites and stories. Others still prefer to be handed their full script and make minor edits. Any of these scenarios can work as long as it is intentional. Your preparation will also depend on your confidence in your communications team and their ability to "get" your voice and the voice of your company. This takes skill and ability to craft the unique angle of the company while also infusing the CEO's voice throughout. Refer back to Chapters 4 and 5 to your Personal Purpose and Company Purpose because this is where you can use those stories, soundbites, and experiences that others can learn from. The most crucial part of your preparation is blocking enough time in your calendar ahead of the event to allow for edits and revisions.
- **Content:** Your content needs to be relevant and real, with a connection to your audience and what they care about. Whether meeting an investor, journalist, or conference organizer for the first time, knowing what content they typically want to know is essential. The following can guide your content creation:

- ○ *Audience:* Who are you addressing, what do they care about, what trends, issues, topics are relevant for them today?

- ○ *Personal history:* Knowing their background and story, where you may have common connections or shared experiences.

- ○ *Reference check:* Who do you know who may know them, what context or history can they share?

- ○ *Prior company connections:* Who do they know at your company today or from the past?

- ○ *Potential angles and questions:* Know the themes of recent interviews, blog posts, social media postings, events attended.

- ○ *Interview content request:* Requested topics or questions to cover. Theme and angle of interview or event.

- **Delivery:** This is where the skill of your live communication is allowed to flourish in the following areas:

- ○ *Convey:* How well you command the physical or virtual conversation, your ability to succinctly get your message across in as few words as possible. Remember:

> **❝**No one will thank you for being verbose.**❞**

- ○ *Captivate:* Whether 1–1, in writing, or in front of a live audience, your ability to enthrall, charm, and woo your audience will get your message across in a powerful way. The prolific use of vocabulary that provokes new thoughts and ideas, the impactful use of silence, pace, and enunciation will help everyone remember you and your company long after you have left.

- ○ *Connect:* The interactive part of any communication with investors, media, or internally is what sets apart the outstanding from the great. Anyone can practice and deliver a well-rehearsed script, but when it comes to the free-flowing interaction and questions, this is where you can build incredible rapport. The idea of practicing extemporaneous conversations is there for a reason at the start of this chapter. It is a muscle you can strengthen, just like learning to deadlift 325 pounds. With the right technique, coach, and practice it is possible, as much as you might think it not to be true right now.

You can now evaluate yourself against the three factors for exemplary executive communication in Figure 9.2. If you have areas you have yet to master, here is what can occur:

1 **Slick, empty words.** Have you ever sat through an interview or conversation wondering exactly what you have been told? This happens when someone has prepared well and delivered flawlessly but their content isn't powerful or memorable enough. Prior to every communication moment you need to ask yourself this one question:

> **"**What three messages do I want my audience to remember?**"**

2 **Fumbled lines:** If you have ever winced on behalf of a presenter who couldn't quite get their words out, this is what happens when delivery is lacking despite ample preparation and strong content. This becomes a huge, missed opportunity as everyone focuses on the style and verbal mishaps and can't absorb the messages. I see this happen far too often in the executive conferences where I often present. There is a misguided assumption from conference organizers that if they review the topic abstract and description for a speaker then they have done their job preparing their audience for an engaging event. The ability to deliver at the right altitude for executive audiences, along with the right level of interactivity, is what sets apart the best executive communicators. It might seem awkward asking a CEO or senior executive for a sample reel, or to complete a dry run-through of their topic, but rather that than an audience of hundreds of disappointed executives reaching for their phones out of frustration that the speaker they came to hear isn't delivering their lines well. You can simply ask:

> **"**Let's run through your content as though I was in the audience.**"**

3 High-stress effort: Personally, with my work with CEOs this is the most common scenario that I experience. With strong content and usually a dynamic delivery, a lack of thoughtful organized preparation creates high-stress moments that are completely avoidable and unnecessary. This is caused by a lack of schedule planning by their executive assistant, not having a strong enough communications guru leading the preparation process, or, for external media, a harried public relations firm that isn't prioritizing the opening night performance for their client.

You can follow the Triple 30 rule for intentionally communicating at every level. If you follow these goals for each of the three 30s, you will calmly get your message across right before the event:

- 30 days prior: the purpose, audience, topics, and messages are clear.
- 30 hours prior: the details, logistics, and script are confirmed.
- 30 minutes prior: your free silent time to prepare.

All of these gaps are fixable and now you can identify which one, two, or three areas you can focus on to improve your executive communications for any audience.

Now you have identified areas you want to improve, and have evaluated which of the external communications mechanisms you may want to stop avoiding and learn how to adore, there are three additional ways to accelerate these.

Reporters

Reporters want to get the inside scoop. It is a misconception that reporters are after a "gotcha!" moment when they are interviewing CEOs. Most want to provide their audience with a chance to understand an executive and their company, not to humiliate them live on TV or to produce a scathing report.

The preparation is critical, but in the moment letting down your guard—of course in an intentional way—is what reporters love the most. Elana Rose, founder of public relations firm The Rose Group, had this advice to share:

> Reporters love to hear a raw moment, a personal anecdote, that leaves them feeling like they learned something new. That they feel like you are being honest and what it is really like to be a CEO of a company right now.

Of course, this isn't random, it is planned, but it is personal. That is how you help reporters build a unique story, because just like a great book, it is the characters that keep you hooked as you form a personal connection to them.

The Amplification of Social Media

Whether you have a love or hate relationship with social media, being anonymous is no longer an option for CEOs and executives who want to rapidly grow their company. I am not going to tell you that you need to start a blog, personally daily posting on social channels that you do not normally hang out on, but you do need to intentionally review your company digital footprint and your personal digital footprint as this can amplify the communication you are trying to achieve. The Executive Social Success Scorecard shown in Figure 9.3 allows you to rapidly evaluate how well you are using the megaphone that is your social channels to your personal and business benefit.

The Executive Social Success Scorecard

As we wrap up this chapter you can now use this tool to evaluate how formed your strategy is, if you have the right resources in place, how current your digital footprint is, how connected you are to relevant social channels, how consistent your content is, how well you are celebrating your achievements, and how proactive you are about building connections. You can complete this scorecard for yourself, for your peers, and for the individuals in your executive team who should also have strong external communications with the media, investors, and the press.

FIGURE 9.3   Executive Social Success Scorecard

	Your Name	Your Peer	Your Team	...	...	...
1. Intentional external media and communications strategy in place						
2. Expert resources in place for content creation, outreach, and posting						
3. Online digital footprint is up to date and relevant						
4. Connected to company, investor, industry, and customer social accounts						
5. Scheduled and spontaneous relevant content is shared						
6. Real-time interaction on posts from investors, industry, customer, and employee content						
7. Celebrate success stories from your investors, employees, peers, customers, and partners						
8. Narrate your daily work, virtual travels, experiences						
9. Actively engage in relevant digital communities with your peers						
10. Identify and approach outlets where you can share your expertise						
Comments:						

Self-assess your Social Success footprint for each of the 10 areas above

I am a role model for my peers

I haven't done this completely or consistently

I haven't done this yet

Communication Lessons from TV Shows

"Don't say that, try saying this.**"**

That is one of the most common phrases I say to CEOs. Sometimes you need to hear how other CEOs and executives talk about their businesses. I suggest these following three television shows because you get to see a wide range of business owners and executives talking about their companies with varying degrees of success. I will often send clips of these shows to an executive prior to an important investor meeting or fundraising round, to then discuss what they saw that worked and did not, and how they can adapt their story and pitch to become more powerful. Here are some TV shows you can learn great communication lessons from.

Squawk Box and Power Lunch

These CNBC shows need to be part of your daily TV viewing. In a matter of minutes or seconds CEOs can tell their story. Watch how they answer questions, how they talk about their business, and what they are being asked about their financials and business strategy.

The Profit

Serial entrepreneur Marcus Lemonis decides which US businesses in crisis he will invest in and then helps them with a turnaround. Of course, there is always some drama to make the show more entertaining, but watch how founders effectively tell their story, share their purpose, and confront what is holding them back. Lemonis is able to cut to the heart of many issues; some founders can handle his direct approach and questioning while others struggle. He will often include fast lessons about profit and loss, costs, and finances, and watch how well those questions can be answered.

Shark Tank

This is the US version of *Dragons' Den*. I met two of the sharks, Damon John and Mr. Wonderful himself, Kevin O'Leary, when I was speaking for CNBC as part of the CNBC Iconic Conference and I am a big fan of this show. They are as charismatic in real life as they are on the show. If you can get over the ego wars, watch how the entrepreneurs pitch their ideas and how good or terrible they are about talking about the financials of their business. A business-changing deal can be won or lost on their ability to communicate their purpose and their profits concisely.

It is a great exercise to set for your team—ask them to watch these shows and then debrief on what communication lessons they learned from the executives and entrepreneurs featured.

The Video Review Everyone Loves to Hate

I have never heard anyone say that they love watching themselves on video. Yet I still keep recommending it for clients I work with. Why? Because it really does help, and you will stand out because nobody likes to do it! I most recently suggested to Kirk Palmer Managing Director Jaimee Marshall that she hold an unplugged, on-camera conversation with francesca's CEO Andrew Clarke, as the search firm supporting a number of executive hires, to capture the essence of the company's growth plans, expectations, and the team they would be joining. I suggested this same video review to Jaimee and Andrew once they saw the first edit of the interview.

The favorite modification I have to reviewing yourself on video is a little strange, but it really does work. When you have a video of yourself to watch, you need to watch it twice. First, turn your computer so you cannot see yourself, but just listen. Pay attention to the actual words you say and how you get your message across. Make notes on what you hear—what you love and what you might want to change.

Then replay your video but mute your sound. Only watch yourself—note how you appear: how do you move, what are your facial expressions, how are you using your hands, if you are on stage how do you move across the stage? You can switch to double speed to watch your entire physical performance in a condensed viewing time if you really want to have some fun, but in all seriousness, it does help you deconstruct the various ways in which you communicate. Send the video to your mentor, strategic advisors, or coach. It is one of the most powerful ways I give feedback to my executive clients if I am not in the room with them for their CNBC interviews, or their CEO conference talks, or their all-hands company meetings, because we can use that video as a way to deconstruct the words that are used and the other elements that enhance or detract from those words to see how well they deliver what they intended.

Now you have evaluated every aspect of your external communications and can see where you have opportunities to improve, let's pause to review what words need to work when you are new in your executive role.

10

Creating Your Perfect Executive Launch

In June 2021, as I was writing this book, a survey from Microsoft revealed that 41 percent of the global workforce is likely to consider leaving their current employer within the next year, with 46 percent planning to make a major pivot or career transition.[1] That means by the time this book hits the bookshelves in January 2022, many of those moves will have happened, generating additional need for comprehensively supporting those new executives, leaders, and teams as they seek to be productive in their new role. That data is backed up by my own research, carried out as I was seeking advice from the executives in my community about which topics they would find most valuable. They agreed that knowing the Words That Work to become successful in a new role or new company was in the top three requested topics. In this chapter you will hear the secrets and disasters from the greatest and the worst executive launches that I have experienced in the last twenty-nine years.

CHAPTER TOPICS

- Why Words Matter as You Launch into a New Role
- First Month Priorities
- First Quarter
- First Year

Why Words Matter as You Launch into a New Role

Why was Amazon able to redefine how designer fashion was sold—encompassing selling cheap socks and books as well as designer handbags, shoes, and clothing? How did Xbox turn a billion-dollar loss into a multimillion-dollar profit machine, resulting in Kinect making it into the *Guinness World Records* for fastest-selling device. How are some CEOs able to take their company through a phase of rapid share growth and position it for acquisition or IPO? What's the common thread? All those companies had to hire and acclimate new executives. It's about how well they can integrate them and keep those people around three months after they join, six months after they join, and many years afterward. Perhaps you are not considering moving jobs but hiring for your team; if so, the most valuable statement you can make to a new hire is this:

"Let's prepare you for your first year on the job."

That is what the most successful companies do. Unfortunately, while best-selling books such as *The First 90 Days* might provide some short-term relief, they create a false sense of security with a quick-fix solution to succeeding in a new role. The reality is you need to focus on Day 365 from Day 1.

It takes one year, sometimes two, to fully integrate and be successful in a new company, but most companies only focus on the first two weeks or on the first ninety days, and then leave leaders, executives, and employees to figure it out for themselves. What you will learn throughout this chapter is what your perfect launch looks like in your first month, in your first quarter, and in your first year. That will give you an idea of the kind of planning and intentional focus that you need to have for your time and your energy to set yourself up for success. Let's start with the top ten Words That Work to use in your first month.

First Month Priorities

1. **"**Here's how I plan to spend my time, energy, and resources.**"**

Exceptional leaders are intentional with their time, energy, and resources. You can use your new role as a chance to press reset on how you work and approach life. You have a seven-day window to set boundaries on where you want free time, work time, and family time before your new corporate calendar takes over like bamboo, expanding into every available gap and taking over the space for other things to flourish. Make the most of the gift of an empty calendar: it won't last long.

2. **"**Let's share our mutual expectations.**"**

This is the time to validate what you discussed in your interview process on strategic priorities, short-term initiatives, financial expectations, and immediate constraints. Understand the external landscape, market conditions, and the competition. Understand how decisions are made and what is valued and rewarded.

3. **"**How do you like to communicate, disagree, decide?**"**

Recently hired leaders who have an open, trusting relationship with their boss deliver results faster and take bold moves to grow the business. Unfortunately, many skip the "so how do you like to work?" conversation until conflict or misunderstanding arises. Proactively ask your chairman or boss what makes them happy and drives them crazy, and then reciprocate. Share with your team. Too many new leaders forget to ask about how someone wants to disagree—is it in public, private, or straight talking at any time? That can make or break your success in your first month.

4. **"Let's discuss the performance and expectations of our board."**

You can use the tools provided in Chapter 9 to evaluate your board, identifying short- and long-term goals. Restate how you will work with them and agree on the frequency and topics you will focus on. If you are in an executive role without regular access to your board, how many clicks away are you? Who represents your work and impact at the board level? How can you increase the visibility of your team's impact with the board? Consider how you are building relationships with key board members.

5. **"Here is what I plan to deliver over the next quarter."**

This is the precise time to declare what you commit to your board and your boss to achieve in your first month, first quarter, and first year.

6. **"Let me spend time sitting alongside every key role in the business."**

Starbucks has every corporate employee spend a week in a Starbucks. When I was working with some of their executive teams, I was impressed that every senior executive knew how to make the perfect cappuccino. That week spent earning their "green apron" gave them that gift as well as insight into life on the frontline of their business. Spend a morning answering phones in customer service, shadow an account executive on a sales visit, or sit through a technical design review.

Identify five areas of your business that you could benefit from seeing from the floor. Meet, shadow, and learn from those people. Do this with curiosity. I recommend that every executive do this.

While you have this gift of an empty calendar, go and answer phones in your customer service center. Go and walk the warehouses during peak times. Go on a sales call with your sales executives. Go to a marketing conference with your PR team. Think of all the various elements of the business that you either know about, would like to know more about, or would like greater context for. I did this when I joined a game studio back in my corporate days, when I was working at Xbox, and in my first week I sat with everybody who did a job that I didn't understand. I sat with the musicians as they were composing music for the games. I sat with the animators, I sat with the engineers, I sat with the artists. I had played video games, but sitting with the creators helped me understand how a video game was put together, including how the flow of building a game worked. This was a small family-run company that Microsoft had acquired, and I went in to manage the post-acquisition integration. But the conversations I had with people about the acquisition—how it was working, what things they wished had happened that hadn't—were incredibly valuable. I built relationships there in my first week that helped me continue to be able to deliver results there. Think about what your thirty days of listening look like. Who can you shadow and where can you be curious in areas of the business that would give you a good understanding?

7. **"I need to prioritize meeting key investors, the board, and my team."**

A new leader's success hinges on the strength of the team they inherit or the speed and effectiveness of repositioning that team and attracting the right talent to deliver their business strategy. Do your due diligence early and thoroughly on what capabilities you need on your leadership team and assess who meets that bar and where you may need to make changes. I have never had an executive reflect that they made leadership changes too fast, only that they regret not moving quickly enough. Trust your gut, test it with specific short assignments (e.g., if you are unsure of someone's strategic ability to think of the long term, ask them to come to you with their top ideas for growing the business for the long term), and then make your decision and move on. Here's another powerful question to ask as you meet with everyone:

"Who else should I meet and can you introduce me?"

As a new executive, you need to quickly build relationships with veterans of the company, and by veteran I don't mean in terms of age or service. I mean people who know the company, the culture, how things used to work, how things work now, and what changes happened. Those are the people you want to build relationships with because they're the people who will help you set up for success.

8. **"What key decisions do I need to make in the next three months?"**

I worked with a company once whose CEO mandated that nobody was allowed to make a decision for the company within the first six months of joining them. So whenever anyone joined, they said, "You can only listen and learn. You can suggest, but you can make zero decisions." It was a great way to force thoughtful learning, but it was a little extreme and did cause a slowness in some product releases that could have been avoided. He had a mandate to try to force people to learn before they acted, and it is an interesting concept to think about. In reality, most companies work at a faster pace than that approach allows for. There is a propensity among executives, especially successful executives who want to prove their worth, to deliver and demonstrate success, but that can lead to decision clash—the number one cause of friction with a new executive. Learn how decisions are typically made and what the preferred preparation for decision-making is. You will need to create decision tenets to reset expectations with your team about when and how you want to be involved in decisions.

9. **"I am currently here on the executive rollercoaster."**

FIGURE 10.1 The New Executive Rollercoaster

New executives' satisfaction with a new role and company is like riding a daring rollercoaster (see Figure 10.1). The timeline in this journey may vary. While I was writing this chapter, one executive told me, "Val, I am already at the 'what have I done?' phase after just thirty days!" Understand from your peers and board what peaks and troughs you can expect and how to continue to lead and influence through them. The greatest risk of an executive leaving is during their first twelve months. A strong inner circle of advisors, clear definitions for success, and a willingness to make and learn from mistakes are three ways to make sure you aren't thrown off track.

10. **"**Here is my Purpose Pyramid, I would love to see yours.**"**

Using the Purpose Pyramid from Chapter 4, you can go deeper to accelerate how quickly your team gets to know you. That will feed your communication and engagement plan with your new team.

First month achievements

By the end of your first month, you should have:

1 A plan for each member of your direct team addressing where you need them to focus in the short term and where you are stretching and growing them.

2 Initial assessment of sales, marketing, product development, finances, customer insight, and strategic options, as well as identification of key questions you need answered.

3 Feedback for your board on expectations and requests.

4 An updated personal growth plan.

5 Immediate tactics in place to accelerate your efficiency (technology, administrative support, logistics).

6 A plan for the speed and sequence for your first quarter.

Use the space below to note your personal priorities.

Your first month focus areas:

First Quarter

1. **"**Here is where I want my team to grow, adapt, and change.**"**

In your first quarter you need to start with evaluating your team. You do that by using the words above to declare how you want to change. Start by looking at the size and scale of your company in three years' time. Then go and hire that team now. In your first quarter it is decision time on your team, moving out those who no longer fit, growing those who have great potential, and developing those who are missing the mark. Once you have your team in place, it is then time to galvanize them. This includes a plan for closing any gaps by building an exemplary board.

2. **"**I have listened, and here are our priorities based on your feedback.**"**

Your assessment in your first month will have informed your plan; next you will identify the speed and sequence of what you tackle, when, and how you are involved. Everyone will want you everywhere or nowhere. You need to decide and inform people how you will work and what you want others to be accountable for.

3. **"**These are the events I am connected to, what did I miss?**"**

Spend time understanding what is happening in your industry and where your company fits in. Get connected to publications, blogs, conferences, and research that inform you and catapult your understanding of your industry's landscape.

4. **"**I want to just validate some details.**"**

Spend time observing areas for yourself. If you are unsure, go and look. Ask questions. Encourage your team to do the same. You will have come to certain conclusions in your first month; how can you test and validate them? You are likely correct, but by observing further you may see different patterns, outliers, examples that give you an even broader level of understanding.

5. **"**Let's discuss where we are going and the path to get there.**"**

At this point you will have enough insights and information to decide how much of a directional change is needed on the strategy. Is it a

U-turn or just a slight bend to the left? Developing this plan and getting your team and board aligned will be the significant focus area in your first quarter. Complete a review of your customer and market strategy with your executive team and board to get aligned.

6. **"I want to validate my observations of how we work around here."**

Pay attention to the culture that you have inherited. How are decisions made? What is rewarded? How are products developed? How is the customer talked about? How does innovation happen? What is the natural speed of the company? How does communication take place? What do you want to keep and what do you want to leave behind?

First quarter achievements

By the end of your first quarter, you should have:

1 A leadership team in place you are confident in.
2 A deep understanding of your industry—your competition, your customers, industry trends and needs.
3 Externally established yourself as an expert in your field.
4 Walked a mile in everyone's shoes—knowing how sales are made, customers are supported, marketing takes place, acquisitions are handled, and new products are developed.
5 Reset the strategy.
6 Identified which cultural aspects need to shift.

Your first quarter focus areas:

First Year

1. **"**Here's what I plan to achieve in my first year.**"**

While it may seem like a distant spot on the horizon when you join, it is important to start planning right away. Your first year will be measured on results, so using these words as your guiding North Star in your first month and first quarter will focus your time and energy. Be clear about what is measured and how you define success. There may be alternative metrics and definitions of success that you want to build in early for your teams and board to start paying attention to.

2. **"**What is the appetite and history for acquisitions around here?**"**

Ask this powerful question to assess the appetite and history for growth. As part of your strategy, you will have outlined your growth goals and approach to acquiring others, IPO, or partnerships. Developing clear criteria with your board for determining and assessing these opportunities ahead of time will help you when the decision needs to be made.

3. **"**I'm proud of the team I have grown and hired.**"**

Executives are assessed against the team they build and grow. Your ability to attract and keep key leaders will be a metric of your success. Create personal goals for each member of your executive team along with a targeted pipeline of future leaders.

4. **"**I'm focused on delivery, delivery, delivery.**"**

Delivering against promises or resetting expectations will be critical in your first year. Identify strategic focus areas, initiatives, and operational requirements, and manage each of them proactively.

5. **"**We are a company where you
can innovate, experiment, and fail.**"**

During your first year you can influence and change the company culture. Put in place a plan for accelerating innovation as a strategic differentiator for your business.

First year achievements

By the end of your first year, you should have:

1 Delivered significant changes to your company's results.

2 Identified who your successors could be.

3 Taken steps to alter the culture to accelerate growth.

4 Become a thought leader in your industry and be called upon for your insight.

5 Strengthened your board to provide insight and direction for the future growth of the company.

6 Reframed the possibilities for the future growth of your company.

Your first year focus areas:

Executive transitions can be tough. They require abundant energy, motivation, and perseverance. Setting realistic expectations that you will go on a rollercoaster ride will help you through the peaks and troughs. Those who quickly deliver results as a new leader show empathy and humility as well as resilience to push the right issues.

Be patient, conscious, and deliberate. Open your eyes and ears and develop a trusted advisor network to help you identify where you are on track and where you need to course correct. Most of all, give yourself time and celebrate the successes along the way.

Now that you have the Words That Work for launching into a new role, I have one final success tip to share that I have seen work incredibly well when an executive switches companies. This tip focuses on your whole life, not just your work life. I explained how you have the magic of an open calendar when you start in a company. You also have another wonderful gift: the chance to reinvent your life. One of the things that many successful executives do when they join a company is to reinvent their lives.

I was just talking to an executive the other day who joined a very big retailer that is growing fast. He said, "Val, I've just started something new. I've decided to incorporate running into my morning routine. So every day now, I run. I go to the office early and I run and then I start my work. It's a new routine I've just decided to implement." He is in the strongest health he's been in for probably twenty years. He decided to reinvent himself. Sometimes external changes allow us to make internal ones that then become visible externally.

I encourage you to think about how you could reinvent your life so that as you move into your new role, you can create a life that you love with the people that you love, doing what you love. I call it being sensibly selfish. Many successful executives sacrifice too much of what they love doing and who they spend their time with. You don't need to do that. You can prioritize yourself, your family, your friends, and fun things by being sensibly selfish. Sensibly selfish means putting yourself first. Treat yourself like your own VIP client, like your own customer. Look after yourself and create a life that you love. The energy that creates will be good for you and for your work.

Next let's explore the playbook that lets you take all these ideas and develop your own reality.

Endnote

1 Microsoft (2021) The next great disruption is hybrid work—are we ready? https://www.microsoft.com/en-us/worklab/work-trend-index/hybrid-work (archived at https://perma.cc/REX5-5BJP)

11

Creating Your Playbook for Success

Business books that explain *what* without *how* do not create the most impact with leaders and businesses. This final chapter dives into just *how* to improve the probability that you will implement what you have learned from this book. It is a rapid-fire collection of tools that successful executives use. It provides secrets for replacing your existing habits with new ones, unlocking new behaviors in your executive team, and learning as you go by implementing, deconstructing, and testing while you are making changes. Complete with success stories from executives around the world who have implemented these tools and ideas, you will go from theory to implementation in record time.

CHAPTER TOPICS

- Ecdysis Evolution
- Vacation Reflections
- Celebrate Memories
- Right Spot, Right Moment
- Teaching Your Executive Team the Power of Deliberate Language
- When You Go Off Track
- The So What Test
- Resistance Is Futile
- Validating Your Success
- Improving the Probability That You Will Act on What You Know

---

If you have read this book in sequence, which is not a requirement, at this point you are likely wondering what you might implement first. There is one important question to ask yourself before deciding to implement anything:

"Does this serve me well?**"**

Ecdysis Evolution

Do you have any idea how often a snake sheds its skin? I was surprised to learn that it is once a month on average. This shedding, also known as ecdysis, is a process that can last between seven and fourteen days. The purpose of the ecdysis is so the snake can keep growing; its old skin doesn't fit it, so it needs to lose it to survive and get stronger. I see the most successful leaders complete their own shedding of what no longer serves them well. You may have already started implementing ideas as you have read through the book, or you may have wanted to wait until the end. This is the point where you can schedule an Ecdysis Evolution of your own. Refer back to your Personal Purpose Pyramid from Chapter 4 and reflect on what you want to shed to make it real. Figure 11.1 (drawing created by Naomi, one of my 11-year-old daughters, and probably one of the most memorable diagrams that I use with executives) shows you the four crucial stages of your Ecdysis Evolution.

Your Ecdysis Evolution

STAGE 1: HABITS
Consider what habits currently do not serve you well and note them below the snake. Add new habits you want to incorporate above the snake, representing the new, stronger you.

STAGE 2: PEOPLE
Next comes my most unpopular but valuable advice:

"Which friends or colleagues do you need to divorce?**"**

FIGURE 11.1   Ecdysis Evolution

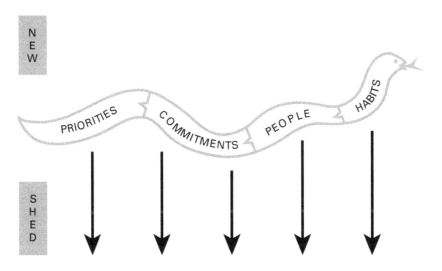

Without overthinking, debating, feeling guilty, or second guessing, write the names of any friends in your life who are not serving you well, do not lift you up, or do not fill you with joy at the thought of spending time with them.

Above the snake, note friends or colleagues you don't spend enough time with—those who already have caused a smile on your face just by thinking of them and the energy they bring to you.

STAGE 3: COMMITMENTS

Then reflect on all of your regular commitments—in your work life, whole life, social life, and charitable life—and note which you want to shed. Consider where you want to add new commitments that will help you fulfill your *raison d'être*. This may take additional thought and time.

STAGE 4: PRIORITIES

Finally, note in the shed zone what your current default priorities have become. Because as work and life become more demanding, there is a natural order to what gets prioritized, even if it is the person or project with the loudest voice or the greatest risk. The opportunity is taking back control of what you prioritize so that you are intentional, or what I call being Thoughtfully Ruthless about what you focus on and when.

Now you can use your insights from your Ecdysis Evolution to make the changes you need.

Vacation Reflections

Another popular tool executives love to use is my Vacation Reflections. I usually send this to the CEOs and leaders I work with on the first day of their vacation. Whether you are on top of the French Alps skiing, lying on a Spanish beach, or road-tripping across Nevada, intentional reflection will help you return to your work refreshed and grounded. Here are the three simple questions I ask:

1 What are you most proud to have accomplished since your last vacation? This can be your mindset, your habits, your relationships, or your business results. Consider your whole life, not just your work life.

2 What has brought you the greatest satisfaction and joy since your last vacation? Get very specific: ask yourself *why* it brought you satisfaction, not just *what* brought you satisfaction.

3 What have you learned about yourself since your last vacation?

I intentionally frame this as "since your last vacation" so that the focus is on recent experience, not old stories and news. It is also a great forcing function to note the frequency with which you take vacations. As a side note, I would like everyone around the world to embrace the European method of vacation, as it boosts productivity. Unlike some countries, the majority of Europeans take a vacation to actually take a vacation, not work from another location, explaining on every call or in every email that you are on vacation but just checking in, or monitoring email. I challenge each of you to make this crucial statement to your team today:

"Vacation Definition: no emails, meetings, or any work.**"**

Your team, and their friends and families, will thank you for it. A further way to embrace the European vacation way is understanding and embracing the fortnight concept. I am not referring to the computer game, but the European name for fourteen consecutive days. It is common to take a fortnight's holiday, fourteen consecutive days away from work. Any European reading this may consider that I am laboring this point, but it is for good reason, because it is such an alien concept that sometimes you have to hear the idea more than once! Even with the recently popular so-called Unlimited Vacation policies, still in the US the time people take away from work is not enough. So add to your playbook prioritizing, taking, and role-modeling for your team the art of taking a long vacation where you do not work.

The next tool for your playbook to accelerate implementation is using your memories to drive celebration of achievements and progress.

Celebrate Memories

"On this day five years ago" is the main reason I stay on social media platforms like Facebook. The memories from this day one, three, or ten years ago are great grounding moments for me. As much as I love looking back at all of the dusty scrapbooks of photos my dad keeps in his garage, it is far more convenient to get a daily digital reminder of years gone by. Sometimes I've even completely forgotten a particular event or moment. I love to end my day checking social media and reminiscing about places, friends, and family from days gone by.

You can add this to your playbook for your work life too.

Jump back in your calendar to this day one year ago. Where were you—who was on your team, what product had you just launched, what challenges have you overcome? You can also proactively set reminders so you memorialize the first anniversary of a product launch, customer success, or financial milestone.

Celebrating your achievements and remembering them keeps you and your leadership team focused on the right spot. There are times when you need to embrace your inner Sherlock and dive deep into solving a challenge, but your default elevation has to be at the right altitude.

Right Spot, Right Moment

For the last decade I have been using the Right Spot, Right Moment framework (Figure 11.2) for defining where CEOs, board members, executives, and their teams need to focus their time. What has evolved in my work with executive teams in the last few years is how this framework flexes depending on the phase your company is in— survival, maintenance, growth, or ownership transition.

You can determine the phase your business is in and map yourself and your team against this framework.

The most powerful statement you can make to your team (depending on the phase) is:

In transition:

"For the next thirty days I will be more involved, then I will back off.**"**

In survival:

"We will all play different roles until we hit this milestone...**"**

In growth:

"It is time to add capacity to our team, let's explore where and how...**"**

In maintenance:

"We need to create predictable success, let's agree who will do what.**"**

In ownership transition:

"We are optimizing for new outputs, here's what is changing...**"**

Teaching Your Executive Team the Power of Deliberate Language

Once you have worked through the Right Spot, Right Moment framework with your team, you will have some immediate insights. Many leaders read my book a second time, skipping to the diagrams and reflection exercises. Another idea is to read it through the lens of each of your team members.

Consider each member of your executive team: who is an exemplar and who has yet to master the power of deliberate language? Consider who can be a role model, and who you may need to provide additional guidance to. A popular event many CEOs run is hosting a book club, reading a chapter of this book each week for eleven weeks

FIGURE 11.2   Focused on the Right Spot at the Right Moment

and discussing it together, providing feedback and advice for each other. Bonus offer: for the first ten readers who text me at www. textvalnow.com with the phrase "Words That Work Book Club," I will attend one of your book club meetings as my gift to you.

When You Go Off Track

Now you have mapped where you and your team will focus, let's have a truth-telling moment:

"You won't always get it right and that is okay.**"**

When I received a call from a flustered executive in Europe last month, I was surprised by just how distraught he was as he usually exudes confidence. I hadn't heard from him in a few years, and he launched into a flurry of examples expressing his concern over a number of mistakes that he wouldn't typically make. He had just walked off stage at his company conference and felt he hadn't conveyed his talk well. But he learned an important lesson that day that belongs in everyone's playbook of success: how to handle failure.

Having someone you trust who you can talk to when you don't get it right is the safety net you need as you take on bigger roles and more responsibility. At that moment I shared with him a story that seemed to help. I said:

> I might have written the *Thoughtfully Ruthless* book about managing your time and managing your resources and keeping up your energy, but sometimes I have to sit down and read my own book! Because life can just take over. I have had to complete my own reflection and find my way back on track to make sure I am fulfilling my purpose as my business shifts back from being 100 percent virtual to deciding how much of my innovation and growth consulting I want to do remotely and how much I will do in person.

That provided the executive with some perspective and caused him to pause and decide to complete his own 5, 4, 3, 2, 1 countdown (Chapter 2) to allow him to reset where he wants to be in a year and his plan to get there. I then shared my favorite quote that I use for moments like this:

> **❝**You are not alone, I see this all the time when…**❞**

The calibration, the pace setting, the acknowledgment that they are not in this alone is often the comfort and reassurance executives need.

The So What Test

Other times we may need a jolt to our thinking with bold questions such as:

> **❝**So what?**❞**

That is what I always like to ask after spending time with a leadership team…

- So, *what will change?*
- So, *what will impact the business?*
- So, *what behaviors and habits need to shift to make that happen?*
- So, *what results will we see having spent time together?*

THAT is where the return on effort and energy is proven.

This is one phrase that some find a little difficult to get used to saying. To overcome the awkwardness of using it, many executives will quote me by saying:

> **❝**As Val would say, so what?**❞**

When you have difficult words to say, quoting others is a powerful tactic to get your message across. This is especially true if you find it challenging to be blunt and direct.

Resistance Is Futile

As we wrap up your Words That Work journey, I want to leave you with a list of typical ways you may face resistance and Words That Work to counter them. A fast guide for your playbook should you encounter them in the future:

No one can make a decision:

> **"**Are we at a point of debate or a point of conclusion?**"**

> **"**Do you have additional questions, or shall I summarize?**"**

Confusion of ownership of a decision:

> **"**Should we involve you throughout, at the decision, or not at all?**"**

Endless discussion loop:

> **"**Let's move on.**"**

Moving from verbose to concise:

> **"**Catch me up in two minutes on the business performance...**"**

> **"**I see your passion for this topic, but what do you need from me?**"**

> **"**Do you have an ask for me or a decision that needs to be made?**"**

"I love listening to your story,
but what is the headline? Let's start there...**"**

"Can I recap? I think I have the
gist, so what do you recommend we do?**"**

Avoiding delay tactics:

"The passage of time won't
change the situation, so let's decide now...**"**

"We have discussed this before,
what are we missing to get to a decision?**"**

"We can't seem to get time to talk
live. Is this no longer a priority for you?**"**

"You seem to be delaying the decision, am I right? If so, why?**"**

Overcoming time black holes:

"We have three decisions to make in this meeting...**"**

"We completed the agenda, we
can all have 11 minutes of time back, bye!**"**

"I can't prioritize that right now...**"**

"What do you hope to achieve in our meeting?**"**

"I have to prioritize my time
effectively; do you have a specific request?**"**

"We need to adjust the cadence of our
recurring meetings together..."

Moving to action:

"Let's do this..."

"Everyone in agreement? Let's go..."

"Any reason not to go ahead now?"

"I am ready to say yes; any disagreements?"

When you are dragged into the tactics:

"How does this contribute to our five-year strategy?"

"Are we all clear what we are optimizing for?"

"Is this what you need to be personally involved in?"

"What role do you play versus your team in this?"

"I don't need this level of detail, neither do you."

"Let's extract ourselves from the tactics."

"Is your team asking you to be
this involved or what is driving this?"

Validating Your Success

Let's take a moment to validate what you have already learned throughout this book.

1 How do I create contagious truth telling?

2 What is the fastest way to deliver results as a newly appointed executive?

3 How can I influence my board meetings to be more productive?

4 How do I improve external media and investor relationships?

5 How do I set the performance bar for my executive team at the right height?

6 How do I know people are telling me the truth?

7 How can I help my team think bigger?

8 How can I test radical, bold moonshots?

9 How do I change my habits rapidly?

10 How do I upgrade my network to the right altitude of peers?

11 How do I rapidly evaluate and change out the right people on my executive team?

12 How do I understand and live my true purpose?

13 How do I help those around me explore new ideas?

14 How do I say what I mean concisely?

15 What are the characteristics of the most successful executives?

Improving the Probability That You Will Act on What You Know

I end every one of my interactive events by asking leaders to write down the number three, three times. The first three is for you to note the three most impactful parts of this book. The second three is for you to share three so whats—how this will impact your business or your whole life. The final three is for you to write down what three actions you will take as a result of reading or listening to this book.

I invite you to text or email me your Triple Three of rapid learning at www.textvalnow.com or val@valwrightconsulting.com. There is a further reason why I am encouraging you to do this. When you write down your action plan, it improves the probability that you will take action. If you share it with another person, it further increases the probability that you will do what you say you will. The final way to improve your success probability is if you take action in the next twenty-four hours. I want you to look at the time, and note your twenty-four hours ticking down like an episode of the famous TV show with Kiefer Sutherland. The safety of the nation may not be at stake, but your ability to communicate your purpose and increase your performance and profit is. So my final words that will work for you are these:

"3...2...1... Let's go!"

APPENDIX

Quotes

Chapter 1

Truth-Telling Words That Work

"I am curious, what prompted you to give me this book? I'd love to hear."

"I'll be blunt, because I know no other way."

"I need your unfiltered advice on this acquisition strategy."

"Does anyone else think we are doing this in the wrong order?"

"Let's pause this conversation to share some inner thoughts…"

"As I listen to you all, it occurred to me…"

"Who wants to go first sharing their observations on this conversation?"

"That felt different from how you typically interact, anyone else see that?"

Preparing the Truth-Telling Conversation

"My intention here is to…"

"Is now a good time to share some thoughts or when would work?"

"Let me be blunt…"

"If I was truth telling I would simply say…"

"I am working on being more direct, so let me say…"

"Does anyone else think we are doing this in the wrong order?"

"I'd love to share my observations, is now a good time?"

Getting to the Heart of the Issue

"I have a contrarian point of view…"

"Does anyone else think we are doing this in the wrong order?"

"Here's how I experienced that…"

"I'd like to share a pattern I have noticed…"

"This is my initial impression, but I thought you would want to hear it…"

"I don't know if you have heard this from others…"

"When is the best time to share some thoughts with you?"

"I have concerns about this project that it is important for you to hear…"

"I have an alternative view to the rest of the team…"

"Before we go ahead may I share an alternative approach?"

"In the spirit of truth telling…"

"As we committed to truth telling, I am going to practice that now…"

"When we were in the last meeting, I am curious how you felt it went."

"I'd love to hear if you thought that conversation went as planned."

"Did you think the team demonstrated truth telling in that conversation?"

"May I share how I observed it?"

Ending the Truth-Telling Conversation

"I appreciate you listening and considering my point of view."

"I appreciate that may have been difficult to hear, but I wanted to share."

If the Reaction to Truth Telling Doesn't Go Well

"I'll give you some time to consider, then let's continue the conversation."

Chapter 2

Setting and Maintaining Performance

"Is this person better than 50 percent of our people doing this job today?"

"What difference would it make if they performed as well as Anita?"

"Performance is contagious, for better or for worse, and you get to decide."

"Do we all know where we are going and how we will get there?"

"Do you have written objectives linked to the company strategy?"

"What do you think is holding back your ability to deliver?"

"What is it going to take for my team to proactively follow up and deliver?"

"What would make the next twelve months your best year yet?"

Preparation for Feedback

"I am curious to understand…"

"Can you see this from a different point of view?"

"It is important to me that I hear your candid reaction…"

"Tell me about your view on…"

Power of Self-Evaluation

"Share how you would evaluate your success in this project…"

"Which functions would rate this a success or room for improvement?"

Probing

"I'd love to hear your reaction…"

"Tell me about your view on…"

"What would you say if you were being really candid?"

"Tell me something that you don't think I'd be aware of…"

"What else can you tell me about..."

"I would love more examples..."

Missed Expectations

"I am concerned you are missing your agreed commitments..."

"It is crucial that you are able to __, and I'm not consistently seeing that."

"Is there anything else that I should be aware of that is causing this?"

"What do you think is a realistic plan to get back on track?"

"What support do you need from me to catch up before quarter end?"

Chapter 3

Getting Others to Cooperate

"Words only work if you say them out loud."

"You woke up today. You are blessed!"

"Physically you might be ok. But internally are you really ok?"

"How does this impact you and how can I help?"

"My hand is on your back."

"I've got your back."

"I think there was some confusion in our objectives here..."

"I have three topics: a, b, and c, is there anything else you want to cover?"

"What is the right frequency we should be meeting right now?"

"Sow the seed, water the seed, walk away, return and harvest the seed."

"I didn't do a good job of explaining..."

"Let me explain the value and impact of this idea..."

"That's a unique perspective, explain more..."

"What do you need from me?"

"I'm having a tough time figuring out how to…"

"I would love to ask for your advice on…"

"I made a mistake and I'd appreciate your help to resolve it…"

"This project is not without risk, I'd love your advice on mitigation on…"

Chapter 4

Creative Internal Communications

"Tell me your story."

"What are your story starters?"

"Tell me one of your inspirational songs that you listen to when…"

"Who do we need to involve before we make the decision?"

"We have made the decision, who needs to help with implementation?"

"Who should we ask to help evaluate how this went?"

Chapter 5

Customers at the Heart of Your Company

"How can we create the unexpected?"

"How can this step be more entertaining and exciting?"

"How can we make our customers more comfortable?"

"How can we throw out the conventional and experiment?"

"How can we ask real questions and get specific answers back that we can act on?"

"How can we provide innovative ways our customers can invest more?"

"How does our customer want to hear from us and how often?"

"What behaviors are important to our customers and how do we improve?"

"What is our intention with our customers and how will we achieve that?"

"If we were a museum exhibit, what would be on display?"

"What do we truly care about and expect of others?"

"Why are we here, why do we matter?"

"Every customer can always…"

"Our commitment to our employees is…"

"We are listening, here is how…"

Chapter 6

It's a Lovely Day for a Moonshot

"We will focus on our known strategies and implement them flawlessly."

"Who do we have internally, and do we even need outside help?"

"As an executive team here's how we will each support this…"

"What has no one else tried?"

"What could be possible and probable?"

"What are we uniquely positioned to create?"

"Which other countries are ahead of the curve on this?"

"If we weren't concerned about failing, what would we do?"

"What is changing in our customers' lives that we can support?"

"What technology exists in other industries that we could use?"

"If we had an unexpected $1,000,000 to invest, where would we spend it?"

"What moonshot stories can you tell where you connected the dots?"

"Who do you know in these companies or industries that we can meet?"

"If you were to reinvent your company today, what would change?"

"What changed at our company during the Covid-19 pandemic?"

Ten Powerful Positive Retorts

Feedback	Positive Retort
"We've tried that before."	"I'd love to understand more..."
"It is just too complex to solve."	"Let's explore what parts are complex..."
"The last three times that failed."	"I'm curious what was different..."
"Our competition doing it faster/better."	"What do they do that we don't?"
"Your assumptions are wrong."	"Let's meet separately so I can hear more..."
"Why are you convinced you can make this work?"	"I'm confident that we can, are you?"
"We are wasting our time exploring this."	"What could we do instead?"
"No one believes this will work."	"For all the same reasons, or different ones?"
"The risks are too high."	"If we overcame them, what is the upside?"
"This isn't the right way."	"Tell me more."

Chapter 7

How to Love Your Anger and Other Emotions

"Be curious when you are furious."

"Do you want help with that, or do you just need to vent?"

"Are you venting and want me to listen, or complaining and want help?"

"I've seen a pattern, you notice what you don't like, but not what you do."

"You were fantastic in that meeting!"

"Take a minute and write down three emotions that are present with you."

"I wish I could take that back!"

"Why don't you share what you are really concerned about?"

"You sound frustrated, what is behind that?"

"Is your concern A or B or something else?"

Challenging Personal Attacks

"Is that feedback you have shared with them directly, perhaps start there?"

"Is your concern with them personally, or the project they are working on?"

"That's harsh, should you really be sharing that with us?"

Sharing Your Opinions

"Here's what I have found from my time here…"

"I've formed this opinion based on the last three projects…"

Testing Unfounded Opinions

"How did you reach that conclusion?"

"What led you to form that point of view?"

"Is that based on what you have observed here or elsewhere?"

Confronting In-Jokes

"That sounds funny, what did I miss?"

Uncovering the Truth

"I get the sense there may be more to understand here…"

"Is there additional context or information that you can share?"

"What am I missing?"

Preventing Radio Silence

"Received, I may need a few days, I'll reply by Friday."

"Received, I have a few competing priorities, I will reply by next week."

"Thanks for your questions, let's schedule a call next week."

Keeping in Touch to Prevent Radio Silence

"I promised to get back to you by _____ but I need a few more days."

"Sorry for the delay, you will hear from me by…"

"I can answer your first question, but let's discuss the others on…"

Breaking Radio Silence in Others

"Can you let me know when I can expect to hear back from you…"

"I'd love to hear from you by x date because…"

"I'd love to hear from you by x date otherwise I will take this action…"

Last Resort on Radio Silence

"It is unusual to not hear back, can you let me know that you are ok?"

Responding to Corporate Buzz Words

"What does that mean to you?"

Advice for Those Who Are Verbose

"Why use a paragraph when a sentence will do?"

"Why use a sentence when one word will do?"

"Why use one word when silence will do?"

Chapter 8

Taking the Boredom Out of Your Board of Directors

"Here is our exit plan and likely time window."

"Let's elevate from the tactics. I really want your advice on…"

"Who do you know in the … space?"

"Be yourself so the people looking for you can find you."

Chapter 9

Turning Investor and Media Interactions to Your Advantage

"External communications are the fastest way to reach your employees."

"No one will thank you for being verbose."

"What three messages do I want my audience to remember?"

"Let's run through your content as though I was in the audience."

"Don't say that, try saying this…"

Chapter 10

Creating Your Perfect New Executive Launch

"Let's prepare you for your first year on the job."

"Here's how I plan to spend my time, energy, and resources."

"Let's share our mutual expectations."

"How do you like to communicate, disagree, decide?"

"Let's discuss the performance and expectations of our board."

"Here is what I plan to deliver over the next quarter."

"Let me spend time sitting alongside every key role in the business."

"I need to prioritize meeting key investors, the board, and my team."

"Who else should I meet and can you introduce me?"

"What key decisions do I need to make in the next three months?"

"I am currently here on the executive rollercoaster."

"Here is my Purpose Pyramid, I would love to see yours."

Words That Work, First Month in a New Role

"Here is where I want my team to grow, adapt, and change."

"I have listened, and here are our priorities based on your feedback."

"These are the events I am connected to, what did I miss?"

"I want to just validate some details."

"Let's discuss where we are going and the path to get there."

"I want to validate my observations of how we work around here."

Words That Work, First Year in a New Role

"'Here's what I plan to achieve in my first year."

"What is the appetite and history for acquisitions around here?"

"I'm proud of the team I have grown and hired."

"I'm focused on delivery, delivery, delivery."

"We are a company where you can innovate, experiment, and fail."

Chapter 11

Creating your playbook for success

Efficiency Improvements

"Does this serve me well?"

"Which friends or colleagues do you need to divorce?"

"Vacation Definition: no emails, meetings, or any work."

The Most Powerful Statement You Can Make to Your Team (Depending on the Phase) Is...

IN TRANSITION

"For the next thirty days I will be more involved, then I will back off."

IN SURVIVAL

"We will all play different roles until we hit this milestone..."

IN GROWTH

"It is time to add capacity to our team, let's explore where and how..."

IN MAINTENANCE

"We need to create predictable success, let's agree who will do what."

IN OWNERSHIP TRANSITION

"We are optimizing for new outputs, here's what is changing..."

When You Go Off Track

"You won't always get it right and that is okay."
"You are not alone, I see this all the time when..."

The So What Test

"So what?"
"As Val would say, so what?"

No One Can Make a Decision

"Are we at a point of debate or a point of conclusion?"
"Do you have additional questions, or shall I summarize?"

Confusion of Ownership of a Decision

"Should we involve you throughout, at the decision, or not at all?"

Endless Discussion Loop

"Let's move on."

Moving From Verbose to Concise

"Catch me up in two minutes on the business performance..."

"I see your passion for this topic, but what do you need from me?"

"Do you have an ask for me or a decision that needs to be made?"

"I love listening to your story, but what is the headline? Let's start there..."

"Can I recap? I think I have the gist, so what do you recommend we do?"

Avoiding Delay Tactics

"The passage of time won't change the situation, so let's decide now..."

"We have discussed this before, what are we missing to get to a decision?"

"We can't seem to get time to talk live. Is this no longer a priority for you?"

"You seem to be delaying the decision, am I right? If so, why?"

Overcoming Time Black Holes

"We have three decisions to make in this meeting..."

"We completed the agenda, we can all have 11 minutes of time back, bye!"

"I can't prioritize that right now..."

"What do you hope to achieve in our meeting?"

"I have to prioritize my time effectively; do you have a specific request?"

"We need to adjust the cadence of our recurring meetings together..."

Moving to Action

"Let's do this…"

"Everyone in agreement? Let's go…"

"Any reason not to go ahead now?"

"I am ready to say yes; any disagreements?"

When You Are Dragged into the Tactics

"How does this contribute to our five-year strategy?"

"Are we all clear what we are optimizing for?"

"Is this what you need to be personally involved in?"

"What role do you play versus your team in this?"

"I don't need this level of detail, neither do you."

"Let's extract ourselves from the tactics."

"Is your team asking you to be this involved or what is driving this?"

"3…2…1… Let's go!"

INDEX

Page numbers in *italic* indicate figures or tables

Printed in the USA
CPSIA information can be obtained
at www.ICGtesting.com
LVHW052042211123
764572LV00004B/4